New Media Careers for Artists and Designers

By

Brenda Smith Faison, Ph.D.

ISBN: 1-4033-5645-9 (e-book)
ISBN: 1-4033-5646-7 (Paperback)

Library of Congress Control Number: 2002093508

This book is printed on acid free paper.

Printed in the United States of America
Bloomington, IN

1stBooks - rev. 01/17/03

A special thanks goes to Gilbert, Valerie and Joyce Faison.

Contents

Chapter I: Job Titles and Responsibilities

What's in a Job Title?

Companies that employ digital artists and designers are particular about how jobs are labeled, and have each developed a jargon with specific descriptions for job titles. This allows each firm to more consistently identify the various disciplines required for jobs. However, according to Cathy McDermott of Computerjobs.com, "even hiring managers out there aren't sure of what exact job titles can attract the right talent that they are looking for." They might come up with a set of proprietary names to use internally, or they may go with those most commonly being used in want ads, and other job postings.

Titles are often selected because they make the job sound more appealing or attractive. For example, animators might be called "3-D Artists." To prevent confusion, most IT websites also have a standard set of titles that they follow. Yet, job titles for new media artists and designers are still evolving. Michael Hoover of Sapient Corporation agrees saying, "I think as people begin to evolve in their roles, you are going to see a lot of roles change titles, and a lot of different roles introduced that didn't exist before." Hoover suggests for example, that the title "information architect" could break down into three important categories. They are: strategy, creative, and technology. He concedes that the market is not there yet, but should be. Hoover's vision of the ideal breakdown involves:

1. Strategy which includes Content Strategy, Content Management, and Brand Strategy
2. Creative comprised of Information Architects and Graphic Designers
3. Technology, including Technical Architects, Engineers, Programmers, and Industrial Designers.

Collaboration and teamwork are standard practices in site development for the Internet. Hoover also listed two groups that currently come together to collaborate on projects. They are:
1. the Creative Group comprised of Information Architects, Graphic Designers, Content Strategy, Content Management, Site Development, and Brand Strategy

1

2. the Technology group with Technical Architects, Engineers, Programmers, and Industrial Designers.

Sites like Computerjobs.com stay active and responsive in staying current with the changing titles by getting feed back from employers seeking creative talent for new media positions. In the digital media arena there are a flood of titles and descriptions from Art Directors to Digital Animators. So, how can the job titles and descriptions in the interactive and digital media industry be systematically categorized and described to bring some consistency and a better understanding to each role?

California's North Valley Private Industry Council (NOVA) developed a more comprehensive list under the auspices of the U.S. Department of Labor. The need for representation on the team may vary depending on the scope and complexity of the project, as suggested by Hoover. NOVA's study contends that a team of interactive digital media professionals could consist of an even greater number of disciplines. In many cases, there are several terms to describe one position. For example: an interface designer might also be know as an information designer, content developer or creative director.

The following is a table of roles and a set of terms they are also known as. NOVA groups them as follows:

Interactive Digital Media Job Titles

1. Producer (Project Manager, Publisher, Production Manager, Director

2. Creative Director (Art Director, Producer, Interactive Writer)

3. Art Director (Creative Director, Producer, Interactive Writer)

4. Technical Director (Lead Software Engineer, Technical Lead, Lead Programmer, Chief Technology Officer)

5. Programmer (Software Engineer)

6. Graphic Designer (Illustrator, Graphic Artist, Multimedia Artist, Web Designer)

7. Animator (2-D) (Production Artists)

8. Animator (3-D) (Technical Director)

9. Interactive Writer (Contents Expert, Author, Multimedia Writer)

10. Interface Designer (Information Designer, Content Developer, Creative Director)

11. Instructional Designer (Information Designer, Educational Designer)

12. Game Designer (Game Producer, Interface Designer)

13. Video Producer (Video Specialist, Video Designer)

14. Sound Designer (Sound Producer, Sound Director)

Core Competencies

Like other industries, there are several core competencies that form the basic skill foundation for all employees. These are in addition to the specific skills that are required for individual occupations.

The list below shows a set of core competencies that every employee in the interactive digital media industry should have. They are:

- Teamwork
- Problem Solving
- Understanding of Production Process
- Understanding of Interactivity
- Communications
- Creativity
- Lifelong Learning

The number one competency according the industry is the ability to work well in teams. This is an industry where virtually all products are produced by teams. The seamless merger between the artistic and technological elements of a project requires input and cooperation from all team members. The popularity of the studio model often means teams are made up of members who may not have worked together previously. This makes the ability to work together with others crucial. As Michael Sherain, an independent producer says, "artists should think of themselves as members of the programming team, and programmers should think of themselves as part of the artistic team."

Another crucial competency is strong verbal communication. Team members need to be able to talk in the other person's language whether technical or artistic. Brilliant programmers and talented artists are not as valuable as team members, if they cannot effectively communicate the constraints that may limit or enable a creative of technological idea. The synergy that results from effective communication often leads to artists inspiring programmers with creative and new ideas, and vice versa.

Incorporating these innovations into the production process requires skilled problem solvers. It is important to come up with a new idea. However, being able to execute it is also a necessary and valuable talent. Since artists and programmers are constantly converting to new tools, critical thinking skills are required to work in this changing atmosphere.

As mentioned previously, the interactive digital media industry is a creative industry that is enabled, not driven, by technology. Creativity and innovation often determine the success of a company and its products. Creativity is essential for all professionals on both the artistic and programming teams.

Another core competency that valued employees should possess is a basic knowledge of the roles and functions of the other team members, and an understanding of the overall production process. Additionally, knowledge of basic business skills, such as budgeting, time management, and organizational capabilities, are valuable. Generally, creative people strive to make each element as interesting as possible, which can be challenging when trying to accomplish a task within an estimated timeline and budget.

In addition to the knowledge of the production process, it is important for all those working in the interactive digital media industry to understand the non-linear nature of an interactive digital media product. It is essential that a professional be able to produce a product with an intuitive and engaging experience for users.

The constant introduction of new technologies and tools demands an enduring enthusiasm for lifelong learning. Employees that are "wedded" to one tool will find their careers dying, as other tools become the new standard. Classes are often created when new tools are released. It is common however, for most professionals to teach themselves a new program rather than attend a class. Therefore, a strong foundation of basic skills will enable people to readily adapt to new methods.

These core competencies interrelate with each other: communication is an essential part of teamwork; creativity is essential to problem solving; understanding the role of others in the production process helps with teamwork; etc. While specific skills are required for each occupation, workers are more valuable if they possess all these core competencies. Here is a closer look at each team member.

Interactive Digital Media Job Titles and Responsibilities

Producer

The Producer is responsible for completing the project on time and within budget, whether she/he originates the idea/vision or someone else does. This involves working with a team on all creative decisions, including the art director, creative director, and technical director. In a small firm, the Producer might handle the Executive Producer's responsibilities as well. These include operations, obtaining deals, and financing. Her/his educational background might include a B.A. or B.S in almost any degree, or equivalent experience. The ideal Producer has experience, a flair for story telling, an understanding of technical capabilities, a strong sense of style, and excellent organizational and motivational skills.

Specific Skills: *conflict resolution, negotiation, organizational and management capabilities, excellent verbal and written communication, established industry relationships, strong expertise in the production process, basic knowledge of the capabilities of software tools and platform constraints, awareness of industry trends, strong visual taste and style, ability to assemble and motivate an effective team of talented people, networked well within the industry with strong knowledge of talented people, and the ability to integrate client requests or technology changes.*

Creative Director

The Creative Director is in charge of the product's overall concept, themes, and ideas. She/he usually works with the Producer to develop the proposal or might accompany the Producer on client presentations. The Creative Director develops the outline or flow of the project, including initial navigation and user interaction design. She/he also assists the producer in writing the creative guidelines for the project. Her/his educational background might include a degree in Art, Communications, English, or equivalent experience. The ideal Creative Director is a talented artist, who can manage, motivate and guide the artistic team, while also having affinity for technology.

Specific Skills: *strong sense of visual style, ability to develop product concept and theme, ability to communicate creative vision to the entire team, strong story telling ability, organizational and management capabilities, understanding of the technical constraints, experience of all phases of the creative process, ability to develop storyboards, ability to communicate with non-artistic* team members, understanding of software tools, and strong written and verbal communications.

Art Director

The Art Director is responsible for the overall "look" or appearance of the product. She/he is generally part of the initial team that develops the overall concept, and assists the producer in writing the artistic guidelines of the project. As the project progresses, the Art Director has responsibility for maintaining visual consistency, and must also manage the artistic team members within the time and budget requirements. She/he works closely with the technical director to keep informed on the newest artistic tools. Typically, the Art Director handles the Creative Director's role as well in most firms, working closely with the Producer. Her/his educational background might include a degree in Fine or Graphic Arts, or equivalent experience. The ideal Art Director is a talented artist, who can manage, motivate and guide the artistic team, while also having an affinity for technology.

Specific Skills: strong sense of visual style, ability to communicate artistic vision to the entire team, organizational and management capabilities, understanding of software tools and platform constraints, experienced in all phases of graphic production, ability to motivate and direct artistic team, ability to develop storyboards, and extensive knowledge of talented freelance artists.

Technical Director

The Technical Director is responsible for the programming and technical aspects of the product. This means developing the programming design to perform in accordance with the technical specifications. She/he will work closely with the Art and/or Creative Director in developing innovative ideas and incorporating new technology. The Technical Director develops the budget and schedule for the programming portion of the project. She/he hires, schedules, and manages the programming team, and oversees user testing. The Technical Director is ultimately responsible for all the company's technology decisions, including software, programming, and platforms. Her/his educational background might include a B.S. in Computer Science, or equivalent experience. The ideal Technical Director relishes technical challenges, makes smart decisions about adopting new technologies, also has a strong visual style sense, and an understanding of the artistic team.

7

Specific Skills: ability to judge when to adopt new technologies, in-depth understanding of the interactivity that technology enables, strong knowledge and experience with various programming languages, e.g. C++, java, etc., excellent communications and management skills, working knowledge of common authoring tools, in-depth understanding of various platform constraints, dedicated to exploring new technologies, ability to communicate with non-technical team members, technical problem solving abilities, and the ability to manage and motivate programmers.

Programmer

The Programmer generates comprehensive designs from product proposals and implements them by coding for appropriate platform and design levels. She/he works with a computer language such as C++, Java or Lingo, and codes, tests, modifies, and documents interactive programs as directed. The Programmer also analyzes, reviews and alters programs to increase operating efficiency or adapt to new requirements. On a lower level, she/he tests product software for "bugs" and suggests changes as appropriate. Her/his educational background might call for a B.S. in Computer Science, or equivalent experience. The ideal Programmer looks for ways to optimize processes and develops assets by leveraging code for a particular project into other uses, as well as understands how artistic elements work with technical elements.

Specific Skills: knowledge of specific programming languages as required for a position, e.g. C++, Java, etc., strong understanding of the theory and logic of computer programming, perseverance and innovative thinking in problem solving, knowing when and how to ask for help, ability to effectively exchange ideas with non-technical team members, and understanding various platforms and delivery medium constraints.

Graphic Designer

The Graphic Designer develops and/or implements the "look" of an interactive digital media project, including: overall graphic design and layout; creation of graphic elements such as templates, menus, buttons, typography; developing the color scheme; and photographic and other image manipulation. She/he may also be responsible for the interface design if a separate Interface Designer is not hired. Graphic Designers are also often called Web Designers when they apply their skill to that medium. Her/his educational background might include a B.F.A. or B.A. in Graphic Design/Fine Arts, or related field or equivalent experience. The ideal Graphic Designer is an individual with strong Fine Art and/or Graphic Design skills who utilizes technology to enhance the user experience.

Specific Skills: solid background in design elements and principles, strong understanding of color theory and typography, strong visual acuity, excellent graphic, drawing, drafting and other art skills, in-depth understanding of most graphic software packages, expertise in selected image manipulation and page layout software, excellent understanding of constraints (limited color palette, bandwidth constraints, etc.), strong understanding of cross-platform constraints, and strong graphic design and layout skills.

Animator (2-D)

The skills classic 2-D Animators have used for years to create cartoons and other media are now being applied to interactive digital media through the use of specialized computer tools. The 2-D Animator will often do many, if not all, of the jobs associated with traditional film animation: character design, storyboard, pencil tests, inking, coloring and in-betweening. She/he will also be working with programmers to implement animations at the code level. Her/his educational background might include a B.A. or B.F.A. in traditional Animation, Fine Art, Graphic Design, or equivalent experience. The ideal 2-D Animator is classically trained, and can quickly learn new computer tools and apply them well in interactive media.

Specific Skills: ability to focus on minute elements, attention to detail, strong knowledge of various illustration and animation software, skill in drawing and classical animation, technical/analytical problem solving ability, good math skills, sculpture skills (for 3-D), understanding of movement and lighting, and excellent visual acuity.

Animator (3-D)

A 3-D animation is started the same way as with traditional methods: with storyboards, character design, etc. Then, the 3-D Animator builds a wireframe model (using 3-D modeling software) that is the object's skeleton. Combined with other models created for background scenery, props, etc. The 3-D Animator programs the model to go through the motions of the scene. The animation is first done on the model before the external features, the textures that cover it, shading, lighting, shadows, etc., are incorporated into the animation, in a process called rendering. Her/his educational background might include a B.A. or B.F.A. in traditional Animation,

Fine Art, Graphic Design, or equivalent experience. The ideal 3-D Animator is classically trained, and can quickly learn new computer tools, and apply them well in interactive media.

Specific Skills: ability to focus on minute elements, attention to detail, strong knowledge of various illustration and animation software, skill in drawing and classic animation, good math skills, technical/analytical problem solving ability, understanding of movement and lighting, and excellent visual acuity.

Interactive Writer

The Interactive Writer assists the Producer in writing and presenting the proposal to the client. Once the project begins she/he works with the client, gathering existing information, data and materials, or performs research to obtain the needed information. The Interactive Writer may also work with a "Content Expert," who has expertise on a particular subject. She/he writes the words that are used in the product, whether they are text that appears on the screen or words that a voice actor will record for inclusion in the audio portion of the product. Essentially, the Interactive Writer creates the "script" used in the project. Her/his educational background might include a B.S. or B.A. in English, Journalism, Communications, or in the field of content. The ideal Interactive Writer has a solid understanding of how to write "non-linearly" for an interactive product, and the ability to write and organize clear, concise copy.

Specific Skills: strong ability to write clear and concise copy appropriate to a specific product, ability to think visually and non-linearly, strong editing skills, ability to organize information, ability to understand target audience, attention to detail, knowledge of English grammar and style guidelines, good verbal communication, working knowledge of the nature of interactive media, excellent research skills, and the ability to adapt writing styles.

Interface Designer

The Interface Designer will often start with a review of what information is to be included in the product, and organizes it in a logical manner that the user will find easy to navigate. She/he then designs the look and functionality of the Graphical User Interface (GUI). The Art Director or Graphic Designer often handles this role, instead of hiring a separate Interface Designer. Her/his educational background might include a B.S. or B.A. in Industrial Design, Human-computer Interface Design, Communications, Graphic Design, a related field, or specialized instruction in Interface Design.

The ideal Interface Designer has an excellent understanding of the nature of interactivity, plus an intuitive knowledge of how a user processes information.

Specific Skills: excellent understanding of theory of human interface design/human learning theory, knowledge of training methods theory, excellent organizational skills, strong understanding of database technology, information mapping ability, understanding of graphic design principles, experience with performing usability analysis, strong understanding of non-linear nature on interactive products, strong capability of programming capabilities, current knowledge of interface design theories, and ability to think innovatively and problem solve.

Instructional Designer

The Instructional Designer works with the client to determine the scope and content of the product. She/he conducts needs assessments, subject matter analyses, and identifies appropriate learning strategies for the content being taught. The Instructional Designer must judge which technologies are best suited for learning a particular topic. She/he conducts usability tests and adjusts the product as needed. Her/his educational background might include a B.S. or B.A. in Instructional Technology, Human-computer Interface Design, Education, or related field. The ideal Interface Designer has a strong understanding of how interactive digital media can create an effective learning process.

Specific Skills: knowledge of cognitive task analysis, knowledge of training methods theory, excellent writing skills, knowledge of learning theory and cognitive science, excellent organizational skills, strong understanding of database technology, information mapping and flowchart ability, understanding of graphic design principles, experience with performing usability analysis, strong understanding of the non-linear nature of interactive products, strong understanding of programming capabilities, current knowledge and instructional design theory.

Game Designer

The Game Designer is responsible for the overall conceptual design of the product. She/he designs the "world" in which the game takes place, as well as the characters that inhabit it. The Game Designer prepares storyboards (often working with a storyboard artist), and flow charts, or "game maps". She/he conceptualizes game story elements into a non-linear format that encourages user interactivity and involvement. At the entry level the Game Designer may be responsible for one section or level of a larger game. Game designers come from a variety of educational backgrounds. Specialized game design courses are now being offered. The ideal Game Designer is exceptionally imaginative, brilliantly innovative, and technologically ingenious. She/he can clearly articulate the game design to the production team.

Specific Skills: ability to conceptualize game story elements into a non-linear format, produce game maps/flow charts, provide expertise in the development of prototypes and end-user testing, in-depth understanding of non-linear nature of interactivity, awareness of artistic and technical developments in the games industry, familiarity with different game platforms, excellent understanding of game theory and play, and the ability to articulate artistic and technical visions to creative and technical teams.

Video Producer

The Video Producer is responsible for all production phases of video elements in the product. She/he shoots original footage or incorporates existing footage into a project. The Video Producer is responsible for the lighting, composition, camera work, and other video production elements. She/he works with the Art Director and/or Creative Director to ensure that the video elements integrate seamlessly with other elements of the product. Her/his educational background might include a degree in Film/Video Production, or equivalent experience. The ideal Video Producer has a strong story telling acuity, and the ability to seamlessly meld video into an interactive product.

Specific Skills: knowledge of different video/digital software, on-line and off-line editing, communications skills, story telling skills, up-to-date knowledge of industry trends, knowledge of composition restraints on computer, ability to shoot video, knowledge of digital compression and other related technologies, understanding of limitations of delivery media, and the ability to integrate video into different media

Sound Designer

The Sound Designer is responsible for all of the audio elements of the interactive digital media product. This may include musical scores, sound effects, and voice-overs. Depending on the size and budget of the product, she/he will either generate or direct the creation of the various elements of sounds. In order to integrate the audio elements into the final product, the Sound Designer will have to utilize programming skills in addition to traditional music composition, etc. Once the various sounds are designed, a significant amount of time and skill are involved in editing the sound into the piece. Her/his educational background might include a B.A. in music, composition, or equivalent experience. The ideal Sound Designer is someone who is creative and innovative in both music composition and sound effects, and can capture the mood of a product.

Specific Skills: *digital recording, audio compression and digitizing, strong composing and music skills, inventive creation of sound effects, working knowledge of current audio software programs, understanding of limitations of delivery media, ability to produce sounds that reflect different moods and emotions, and ability to match style of sound to nature of the product.*

Animation and Digital Effects

The animation and digital effects industry also presents a significant number of opportunities for artists and designers. Both animation and digital effects are sub-sectors of the entertainment industry. Animation and digital visual effects were used extensively in the production of some the top grossing films in history, such as *Jurassic Park, The Lion King,* and *Independence Day.*

The animation and digital effects industry segmentation is broken down into two groups: 1) Process: Animation (traditional and digital), and Visual Effects (digital); and 2) Medium: Film (features – live action, animated, and hybrid and shorts; Television (shows – live action, animated, and hybrid); and commercials; and On/line Interactive (commercials and trailers, and websites.)

A summary of traditional animation process includes ten-steps where the script is written, a storyboard is created, scene layouts are developed, key frames are animated, intermediate frames are animated, in-between frames are animated, backgrounds are painted, cels are painted, cels and backgrounds are assembled for photography, and painting and color integration is done electronically with computers.

Digital visual effects processes comprise eight steps including: visual development, storyboard, research and design (R&D), modeling, animation, lighting, compositing, and film/video.

Animation and Digital Effects Job Titles And Responsibilities

Jobs in the animation and digital effects industry are organized into job families. The family framework of occupations in Digital Visual Effects, traditional and computer animation are as follows: 1) Visual Development, 2) Story (storyboard), 3) Layout, 4) Painting, 5) traditional animation, and 6) Computer Art. The traditional animation family includes two sub-families: Character/Effects and Clean-up.

The computer art family includes three sub-families: 2-D, 3-D, and Technical. The following are titles and descriptions specific to the animation and digital effects industry.

Visual Effects Supervision

A job in this family, explores literary or musical property to develop the story and its components. The Visual Effects Supervisor supervises all of the special effects operations of a film. She/he works closely with the director in planning all visual effects and is responsible for ensuring that the intended aesthetic of the director is realized. The Visual Effects Supervisor oversees, coordinates, and manages the work of visual effects personnel and the visual effects artists (Compositors, 3D Artists, Senior Artists, etc.).

Specific Skills: The Visual Effects Supervisor should have a clear understanding of the artistic skills and capabilities of the various personnel in the visual effects process. The Effects Supervisor will also have an integral understanding and knowledge of the technical skills required of the various personnel involved in the visual effects process.

Visual Effects Development

The Visual Effects Developer conceptualizes a scene and expresses it artistically. She/he works with the director, producer, and writer. This is in contrast to Character and Effects Development Artists and Designers, whose skills are similar but are in these specific areas.

The ideal Visual Effects Developer is experienced with working with managers at higher levels, as well as deadline management, completing tasks independently, client interaction, and teamwork.

Specific Skills: The Visual Effects Developer's artistic skills includepainting, drawing, story development, artistic style, imagination (the same as the traditional animation skills for

14

character and effects development artists and designers). Her/his technical skills comprise the full range of 2-D and 3-D software.

Animation and Digital Effects: Storyboard

Storyboard Artist

The Storyboard Artist interprets scripts to create storyboards and plans shots. She/he visualizes and conceptualizes the story before drawing it, incorporating different angles, and maintaining continuity among the shots. Typically, the Storyboard Artist needs one to two years of experience for this job.

Assistant Storyboard Artist

The Assistant Storyboard Artist does more developed clean-up, and begins to prepare some sections of the storyboard under supervision. Typically, she/he needs six months to one year of apprentice experience for this job.

Apprentice/Clean-up Storyboard Artist

The Apprentice or Clean-up Storyboard Artist revises storyboards, including dialogue and characters.

The ideal artist in this family has developed such organizational skills as following directions, completing tasks independently, as well as management and delegation as the job level advances.

Specific Skills: Artists in this job family have artistic skills that include following a style, cutting and pasting, drawing and quick sketching, basic backgrounds (buildings, landscapes), perspective and composition, cartoon and realistic drawing styles, story development and interpretation, conceptualization, and understanding the animation process (script timing, next step layout). This family of artist display technical skills that include basic computer literacy, and storyboard software.

Animation and Digital Effects: Layout

Artists in the Animation and Digital Effects: Layout family break down a storyboard and stage every scene and camera set-up through drawings. She/he will progress from lower-level to higher-level jobs on the basis of skills and experience.

Layout Artist

The Layout Artist will stage every scene and camera set-up through drawings. She/he draws backgrounds and characters, and understands the animation process. Typically, The Layout Artist needs three to five years of experience for this job.

Key Assistant Layout Artist

The Key Assistant Layout Artist plans scenes and makes camera movement decisions.

Apprentice/Clean-up Layout Artist

The Apprentice/Clean-up Layout Artist finalizes the backgrounds by cleaning up lines before passing them on to the background painter, or for scanning.

The ideal artist in this family has developed such organizational skills as teamwork, following directions, deadline management, completing tasks independently, and management and delegation as the job level advances.

Specific Skills: Creatives in this job family have artistic skills that include cartoon drawing, following basic designs of established characters, and understanding how scenes work. Technical Skills such as camera mechanics (including field size and camera movement), and painting software (for computer layout artists) are also required.

Animation and Digital Effects: Painting

Painters must be trained in Fine Arts Painting for a job in this family. Typically, she/he will start as an assistant background painter, then progress to the next job level of Background Painter, on the basis of skills and experience. If she/he works as a Matte Painter, then advancement in skills and experience is gained, yet, there is no job level advancement.

Background Artist

The Background Artist designs backgrounds based on the layout drawings, working with the Layout Artist. The amount of drawing and design depends on the layout detail. She/he determines the medium for translating the drawings into color.

Assistant Background Artist

The Assistant Background Artist uses various media to paint backgrounds under the supervision of the Background Artist.

Matte Painter

The Matte Painter works in a visual effects company painting imaginary or inaccessible scenes for live action features.

The ideal artist in this family has developed such organizational skills as following directions, deadline management, completing tasks independently, and teamwork.

Specific Skills: Creatives in this job family have artistic skills that include painting in various media (photo realism), artistic style, and drawing; and have basic technical conversancy.

Animation and Digital Effects:
Traditional Animation

Character/Effects Animator

Animators in this subfamily work on the cel animation of characters and effects, and generally progress from lower-level to higher-level jobs on the basis of skill and experience.

Supervisory Animator

The Supervisory Animator works with the Director to manage the overall animation process.

Animator

The Animator develops characters. This job has been described as "acting with a pencil."

Assistant Animator

She/he interprets the animators' rough drawings, leaving a few frames for the In-between Animators. This can be a career position without further progression.

In-Betweener

The In-Betweener fleshes out the movement of animated sequences by providing "in-between" drawings as specified by the Assistant Animators and the Animators.

The ideal candidate for this subfamily in a creative who has developed the ability to follow directions, complete tasks independently, work on a team, and manage and delegate as the job levels advance.

Specific Skills: Creatives in this job subfamily have artistic skills that include a strong understanding of color, perspective, design and lighting theory, following a style and drawing clean lines (for in-betweeners). Acting, timing, drawing characters, solving proportion problems (for character animators); atmospheric rain, dust, shadows drawing, and ability to make the characters' world real (for effects animators are also required). Technical skills requirements include basic computer literacy, and camera mechanics.

Animation and Digital Effects

Traditional Animation: Clean-up

This subfamily, works on cel animation clean-up only for major feature productions. Usually, progression from lower-level to higher-level jobs is made on the basis of skill and experience.

Key Assistant Clean-up Artist

The Key Assistant Clean-up Artist works with the Animators, manages the clean-up process, breaks down work into scenes, and delegates them to the Assistant Clean-up Artists.

Assistant Clean-up Artist

The Assistant Clean-up Artist manages whole scenes, breaks them down into sequences, and supervises the in-between clean-up artists.

In-Between Clean-up Artist

The In-Between Clean-up Artist provides detailed drawings of rough drawings made by the animators under the supervision of the Assistant Clean-up Artists.

The ideal candidate for this subfamily in a creative who has developed the ability to following directions, complete tasks independently, work on a team, and manage and delegate as the job levels advance.

Specific Skills: Creatives in this job subfamily have artistic skills that include basic drawing, drawing with high line quality and consistency, figure and anatomy drawing, and flipping. Technical skills requirements include following exposure sheets, and following and directing timing charts.

Animation and Digital Effects: Computer Art: 2-D Animation

This subfamily creates 2-D artistic elements using computers, and are not organized by levels. Usually, these jobs allow for advancement in skills and experience without moving into a different job.

Painter

At the entry level, the Painter applies color to objects and removes wires and props. She/he may also do some basic rotoscoping. After gaining significant experience, the Painter does color modeling and creates color keys that an entry-level Painter applies. She/he works closely with the producer and art director.

Ideally, Painters have developed organizational skills ranging from following directions, teamwork, deadline management, client interaction and completing tasks independently, to management and delegation as required.

Specific Skills: *Painters are adept at tracing on film and the computer, and have developed technical skills using painting software.*

Rotoscope Artist

The Rotoscope Artist creates mattes by isolating the elements of frames to modify or remove them. At the entry level, she/he begins with elements like dirt and wire removal. Ideally, the Rotoscope Artist has developed organizational skills ranging from following directions, deadline management, client interaction, completing tasks independently, to management and delegation as required.

Specific Skills: Rotoscope Artists *are adept at painting and drawing, and have developed technical skills using painting software.*

Texture Painter

The Texture Painter creates the map, which is a 2-D skill, and then applies it, which is a 3-D skill. The same person often performs these tasks.

Ideally, the Texture Painter has developed organizational skills in deadline management, and completing tasks independently.

Specific Skills: *Texture Painters are adept at painting, and have developed technical skills using painting software.*

Compositor

The Compositor uses software to layer and match several images in a frame. Ideally, the Compositor has developed organizational skills ranging from following directions, deadline management, teamwork, and completing tasks independently, to management and delegation as required.

Specific Skills: Compositors are adept at matte logic, lighting, photography, composition, perspective, and have developed technical skills using related software.

High Speed Compositor

The High Speed Compositor works directly with clients doing real-time compositing. She/he handles long shots and final overall fixes.

Ideally, the High Speed Compositor has developed organizational skills that include teamwork, dealing with pressure, and client interaction.

Specific Skills: High Speed Compositors are adept at lighting, photography, composition and perspective, and have developed technical skills using compositing software.

Animation and Digital Effects: Computer Art: 3-D Animation

Computer Art: Technical

Positions in this subfamily allow for the creation of artistic elements using computers, and are not organized by levels. Usually, these jobs allow for advancement in skills and experience without moving into a different job.

Match Mover

The Match Mover uses animation software to match the positions of 3-D computer graphics databases, i.e., a model, into something that was already shot in live action. Ideally, the Match Mover has developed organizational skills such as deadline management, communication, and completing tasks independently.

Specific Skills: The Match Mover position requires no artistic skills at the entry level, however, technical skills both analytical and detail orientated are required.

Motion Artist
The Motion Artist designs technical specifications of characters' movements, and creates proper computer controls to enable movement. She/he works closely with Computer Animators. The ideal Motion Artist has developed organizational skills such as teamwork, deadline management, and completing tasks independently.

Specific Skills: The Motion Artist is adept at animation that includes 3-D motion and structure; and has a strong understanding of the human anatomy. Her/his technical skills include Animation, 3-D motion and structure; and human anatomy.

Lighting Artist
The Lighting Artist positions lighting and sets the mood for scenes.

The ideal Lighting Artist has developed organizational skills such as teamwork, deadline management, and completing tasks independently.

Specific Skills: The Lighting Artist is adept at photography, film and set lighting, and has a strong understanding of the human anatomy. Her/his technical skills include 3-D software, and detail orientation.

Shader Writer
The Shader Writer writes RenderMan™ shaders to help create the look of the film, and the physical properties of the objects being lit.

The ideal Shader Writer has developed organizational skills such as teamwork, deadline management, and completing tasks independently.

Specific Skills: The Shader Writer is adept at animation, composition, lighting. Like the Lighting Artist, the Shader Writer is also proficient with photography, film and set lighting, and has a strong understanding of the human anatomy. Her/his technical skills include programming in C, rendering software, and detail orientation.

Effects Animator
The Effects Animator uses 3-D painting software, such as Wavefront™ or Prizm™, to model natural phenomena.

The ideal Shader Writer has developed organizational skills such as file management, deadline management, teamwork, and completing tasks independently.

Specific Skills: The Effects Animator has developed artistic skills in movement and perspective with technical skills including high-end software, and programming.

Animation and Digital Effects: Computer Art: 3-D

Positions in this subfamily allow for the creation of 3-D artistic elements using computers. These positions are not organized by levels. Creatives are likely to advance in skills and experience without moving into a different job.

Modeler

The Modeler uses software to create 3-D models, and has an understanding 3-D space and perspective. The ideal Modeler has developed organizational skills such as deadline management, teamwork, and completing tasks independently.

Specific Skills: The Modeler has developed artistic skills reading blueprints, and traditional modeling, i.e., sculpture. Her/his technical skills include 3-D software, and production.

Animator

The Animator uses software to create and animate characters, objects, or effects, and is responsible for choreography, timing, and acting of characters, objects, or effects. At the entry level, she/he animates simple characters. After gaining significant experience, the animator takes on more complex shots. She/he may also manage people.

The ideal Animator has developed organizational skills such as file management, deadline management, teamwork, and completing tasks independently.

Specific Skills: The Animator has developed artistic skills in animation, including traditional characters, 3-D motion, 3-D structure, and life drawing. Her/his technical skills include animation software; programming skills are also helpful.

Layout Artist

The Layout Artist blocks, stages, and does camera set-up for every scene. The ideal Layout Artist has developed organizational skills such as file management, deadline management, teamwork, and completing tasks independently.

Specific Skills: The Layout Artist has developed artistic skills in drawing, design, and understanding how scenes work. Her/his technical skills include 3-D modeling software, graphics software, Unix lighting software, detailed multi-tasking software, a B.A. level knowledge of computer science, and production.

Animation and Digital Effects:
Computer Art: Technical

Jobs in this subfamily allow for the creation of artistic elements using computers, and are not organized by levels. Creatives are likely to advance in skills and experience without moving into a different job.

Match Mover
The Match Mover uses animation software to match the positions of 3-D computer graphics databases, i.e., a model, into something that was already shot in live action.

The ideal Match Mover has developed organizational skills such as deadline management, communication, and completing tasks independently

Specific Skills: The Match Mover position requires no artistic skills at the entry level. Her/his technical skills are analytical, and involve detail orientation.

Motion Artist
The Motion Artist designs technical specifications of characters' movements and creates proper computer controls to enable movement. She/he works closely with Computer Animators. The ideal Motion Artist has developed organizational skills such as teamwork, deadline management, and completing tasks independently.

Specific Skills: The Motion Artist is skilled in animation, including 3-D motion and structure, and human anatomy. Her/his technical skills include 3-D software, and detail orientation.

Lighting Artist
The Lighting Artist positions lighting and sets the mood for scenes.

The ideal lighting Artist has developed organizational skills such as teamwork, deadline management, and completing tasks independently.

Specific Skills: The Motion Artist is skilled in photography, film, set lighting. Her/his technical skills include 3-D software, and detail orientation.

Shader Writer

The Shader Writer writes RenderMan™ shaders to help create the look of the film, and understand the physical properties of the objects being lit. The ideal Shader Writer has developed organizational skills such as teamwork, deadline management, and completing tasks independently.

Specific Skills: The Shader Writer is skilled in animation, composition, lighting, and artistic skills of a lighting artist. Her/his technical skills include programming in C, rendering software, detail orientation.

Effects Animator

The Effects Animator uses 3-D painting software, such as Wavefront™ or Prizm™, to model natural phenomena. The ideal Effects Animator has developed organizational skills such as file management, deadline management, teamwork, and completing tasks independently.

Specific Skills: The Motion Artist is skilled in photography, film, set lighting. Her/his technical skills include 3-D software, and detail orientation.

Shader Writer

The Shader Writer writes RenderMan shaders to help create the look of the film, and understand the physical properties of the objects being lit. The ideal Shader Writer has developed organizational skills such as teamwork, deadline management, and completing tasks independently.

Specific Skills: The Shader Writer is an expert at movement, and perspective. Her/his technical skills include High-end software, and programming.

Chapter II: The Role of the Creative

Artists and Designers or IT Professionals

With so many artists and designers working in the digital realm of interactive multimedia and animation, disciplines often overlap and blur the distinction between art and technology. The term "IT Professional" (information technology professional) often conjures up a vision of old Cobol coders or C++ programmers, and often means different things to different people. Visual/graphic designers for example, are involved in structuring information, and shaping graphical and textural content that the audience sees on screen. Digital artists and designers use their craft for the evolutionary development of IT. They are highly specialized information technology professionals.

Such a position might call for strong aesthetic sensibilities, skills in information design, as well as HTML programming, the ability to code simple Java, etc. Artists and designers play a key role in the success or failure of the end product through the application of design elements and principles that have been used by all types of artists over the centuries. In new media, the tools are digital and the canvas is the screen, the creative's imagination and creativity transfers, and is critical to the success of the end product.

Artists and designers mask much of the complex coding, so the masses will be driven to and enabled to view, navigate, and pleasantly experience the digital product in an engaging, visually stimulating, and user-friendly manner. "There are all types are IT professionals out there", according to Cathy McDermott. of computerjobs.com Some are writers, hardware specialists, information systems specialists, programmers, tech recruiters, project managers, personnel managers, even IT executives; all with knowledge at different levels." McDermott believes IT professionals do include artists and designers with various levels of artistic and technical knowledge, and organizational skills. Their roles are also crucial to the realization of the final product, as are those of the programmer or engineer.

The final distribution point might be the Internet, CD ROM, video, film, etc., and the goals are optimum user experience and the effective visual communication of graphical, textural and numerical information. Jackie Dane of iXL Enterprizes, Inc. agrees saying, "designers shape what you see on the Internet, the content." Their contribution, the tools, and their vital impact on the success of the final product place creatives under the information technology professional umbrella as well.

The Evolution Of Designers' Roles

The project team is generally interdisciplinary, involving members with a variety of skills and disciplines. The team may comprise designers involved in a variety of crafts from graphic design to animation and video producers, who work with programmers, human factors content researchers, writers, etc. The role of creatives on the team has increased in value as aesthetics and ease of use have become a large part of the success of various digital applications.

According to Eileen Matis of Rare Medium Group, Inc., the previous perception was that hard-core Programmers held a more prominent place in the development of a product. The interdisciplinary team approach gave artists and designers a chance come to the table at the beginning and stay involved throughout the development of a project. Additionally, it allowed creatives to showcase their skills, gain knowledge of other disciplines, and prove how essential the visual and navigational component was to the survival and continued effectiveness of the product. Today, these creative artist and designers have raised the bar to a level of quality and excellence that is accepted as the norm, and current applications are judged by these standards. In developing a new application, few established groups, firms, or organizations would overlook the artist and designer as a standard resource.

Matis views design as "the culmination of visual aesthetics, combined with information architecture, and in many cases, user experience architecture to develop the entire user interface." Designers are more vocal in speaking out about the importance of good visual aesthetics and user experience. Designers like Aaron Marcus of Aaron Marcus + Associates, Clement Mok, Chief Creative Officer at Sapient, and Lynda Wienman of Lynda.com have led the way.

Also, each firm or group would have a development process that varies from one team to another. Here is one scenario suggested by Jackie Dane of iXL Enterprizes, Inc. She notes that the diversity of the development team depends on the needs of the project, yet there is always someone from visual design, programming, information

27

architecture, and human factors on the team. The project would also determine the number of members from a particular discipline versus another, because there may be more of a need in one area than another. For example, a project involving a great deal of visual content, might require more artist and designers on the team. There might be people doing graphic design, animation, shooting and editing video, etc.

"It's important that we all work as a team to make sure we're communicating the right concepts; the creative director leads this process." Within the creative group there are creative artist, art directors, graphic designers, as well as production designers. There are also information architects, usability engineers, interface developers, and software engineers. There are several other support groups available that support us in terms of industry practice and knowledge, research groups, etc.

The Creative Services Group at iXL has client contact and helps the client understand the subtle nuances of their competitors' site, based on the brand they want to convey, not simply the functionality of the site. They might note the use a similar palette, or a similar use of imagery, for example. This helps the client understand what their competitors are doing. They work to understand the client's own particular message, looking at their competitors visually and finding out how they convey their message and what the competition actually looks like.

It is important for the creative group to bring this content to the team, so that the information architects and Web developers can reference it. In the team's brainstorming sessions, a programmer may know about a new technology that someone else on the team may not be aware of, and can contribute that. A variety of ideas are suggested by all members, regardless of their discipline. In this phase, contends Dane, "the role that the designers play is not so much creating artwork, but taking a creative approach to the problem solving." This might also involve bringing and element of fun to the process, leading brainstorming sessions, sketching out ideas for screens, etc.

The designers support the creative director's role in coming up with a visual strategy. The Creative Group gets together to look at the competition. They put all their samples up on a wall, and analyze and discuss all those companies that are direct competitors of the client, and/or perhaps just some firms within the industry that are conveying messages or using media similar to those Dane's client wants to incorporate.

Simultaneously, the information architects and usability specialists are doing user research to find out what the needs of the user are, and to evaluate, document, and analyze the content. They do this by working on lists of content, and content matrixes to learn what the content should be in that title or site.

Dane continues, "once we have the creative strategy together, we usually present it to the client for input in an effort to determine if the client agrees." The team checks with the client on such things as current status, where they need to be, and what their competitors are doing. "This allows the client to see where we are headed before we begin to develop the screens," says Dane. Later, if the client does not like a screen, it gives her/him a better context in which to give input, and makes the process less subjective. This also gives the information architect a little more headway when developing navigation and flow of the content.

Once a creative strategy is developed, screen designs can begin before all the navigation done. Then, the creative strategy is presented to the client; the information architects are present the whole time. "Even though we all have a lot of work yet to do, we're getting a portion of our piece done at the same time," says Dane who reviews the full brief of the entire team before she presents it to the client. Much of what information architects are doing initially is making lists and working on functional requirements documents.

At some point, the Creative Services Group and the information architects have a workshop were they again meet with the client and go through the functionality issues, prioritize what should come in the first phase, second phase, third phase, etc. In that workshop, they may decide if there is some other industry leader who should be present in order to give greater context to the current research. At this point, the designers have begun to come up with a visual strategy, though they have not yet delivered it. So, designers are in these workshops where the functions are being prioritized, and can give their input based on what they have seen. They are also understanding what the rest of the team is doing in terms of the functionality and technical specifications.

Once the information architects come up with a hierarchy or flow of the site, a file is developed for every screen. Within some screens, there may be additional artwork. The production artist or digital illustrators work to create and develop all the elements that go together in the interface.

"This level of participation, involvement, and contribution is a far cry from the time when designers were given whatever type of information or existing collateral on behalf of the client", says Dane. With a limited set of project specifications, they were told to "go off and do their thing." As Dane and Matis remind us, design is not just making pretty pictures.

Fewer Limitations

With the process today, creative consultants, artists and designers are not limited to visual aesthetics alone, but are responsible for the delivery of a variety of creative elements of a project. "Every discipline on the team is responsible for a set of deliverables," says Dane. However, all deliverables are seen as team deliverables that enables all team members, regardless of their discipline, to comment on each other's work.

Therefore, the whole team is viewed as experienced information technology insiders, and all views or opinions are considered. Digital designers in collaboration with this interdisciplinary team, develop visual concepts, strategy, address navigational schemes, and work together with clients to determine who they want to be. They are solving problems and work interactively throughout the life of the development of the project. "It is a true team effort", according to Dane.

Additionally, McDermott notes, "many designers also have advanced degrees in the areas such as user interface design, web navigation, computer graphics technologies, etc.," and are conversant on related topics that go beyond visual effects. She feels if designers are relegated to only establishing the look and feel of a site or title, then they are being cut off from being a more valuable, contributing member of the team.

Client Contact

Historically, traditional ad agencies were very big on a hierarchical system in which only certain people (usually account representatives) were client-facing and collected information from the client or customer. Then, everybody else just took the given information from the account manager, and worked from that. According to Hoover, Sapient has always been big on the idea that "regardless of who has contact with the client, you are involved in understanding what the client's problem is; otherwise, you're just reading it from a document." So, communication skills are definitely important for artists and designers.

Dane agreed that client contact was desirable, but with more structure. It is the creative director and art directors who typically interact with the client and are very good at explaining a concept and extracting ideas out of client discussions. She explains, "some designers don't wish to be a director. They are very good at design; and that's what they want to do design." She insists that this does not hold them back in their careers saying, "they can become masters and experts in design, but they will always be doing design."

However, all team members are present for presentations and can question the client. This usually depends on their personality, comfort level, or confidence. Typically, the creative director and the art director make the presentation. According to Dane, if there is a particular piece that was done by a specific designer, "depending on the individual, the client, and the dynamics of the group; the designer might also present to clients."

Success of the End Product

Certainly, every discipline involved in new media title and site development would argue that the contribution of their discipline group makes the greatest contribution to the end product. The strongest argument I found came from Jackie Dane. She explains it this way,

> "Visual interface design <u>is</u> what gives the impression to your user. That is your sole communication with the end user; what they see is what you are. That said, you might think that means it is the most important thing..."

On the other hand, Dane also admits that in order to have a good visual interface design, you need a well-developed information architecture, a well-developed set of functions, and a well-developed understanding of your brand and user. She further explained,

> "It is of utmost importance that the visual interface designers involve themselves in all the steps in the development of each of those areas. This helps them to fully understand them. It is up to them [the

31

> *designers] to communicate it correctly. So, it's sort of*
> *give and take. I would say it is very, very important."*

Matis feels the artist and designer were highly instrumental in the success of the final product. She recalled the non-sence of error messages of first generation Web sites where usability found little attention, and she thought, "eew, there's technology involved here!" She feels if visual designers, graphics designers, and information architects were taken out of the picture, we would have is an Internet filled with white, text-filled pages such as those of those first generation sites. She also noted,

> *"You had a lot of words that meant nothing to the*
> *average individual, unless they were 'in the know'.*
> *You could scroll for days and still not get what you*
> *were looking for. So, the visual designers, and*
> *information architects are extremely critical to the*
> *success of new interactive products."*

Percentage Attributable to Artists and Designers

Could the contribution of Artists and Designers be broken into percentages? Not accurately. The team approach to development, and the variables of each project makes an accurate percentage almost impossible to establish. Matis found her environment more server-centric, and could not give you exact range. This is because certain projects require lower levels, where other projects require massive levels of input from creatives. She did estimate a range of between 35% to 100%, adding, "some projects straight creative. We do projects that are a true marriage between the creative side and the server side, meaning 50/50 on each part, while other projects are 65 sever-side and 35 client-side." As an end-to-end solutions provider, Matis finds it an exceptionally broad range with too much variance to divide into exact percentages.

A client might only need one component. They might have developed their server-side technologies in-house, and had no designer available to bring them to the Web in a manner in which they need to be portrayed. So, they would call on an Internet development firm. Or, 100% might be done by the firm. Matis believes this variable might hold true for similar firms as well.

At computerjobs.com, McDermott explained, "all new products on some level touch the hands and minds of the creatives, particularly if it goes external." Hoover agreed saying 90% of his clients would require creative services. He explained, "in some form or another, they should touch the hands of a designer. It may not be as intimately in some cases as others, but there definitely will be a sign-off." This is particularly true with branding, etc. Essentially, Sapient develops products for the Internet, whether it's business-to-business, or business-to-consumer; Hoover believes, "it involves graphic designers in the interfaces that people are seeing and interacting with out there."

Dane believes it is more than 50%. Yet, also admits it's hard to say because of the dependency of one group or discipline on another. "You can have a great design, but if the navigation is flawed, it's supporting poor navigation," reminds Dane. Communicating the message goes beyond just the "look" of a product.

As a consultant, Matis thinks all of the involved disciplines are crucial and it is the responsibility of everyone on the team to do their best, regardless of their dicipline. She noted,

> *"If you feel the visual interface design is not a success for the client, though you may be an engineer; it's still your responsibility to say something to the rest of the team. Especially if you feel it should go in another direction."*

On the other hand, Dane feels it is up to the creative staff to get buy-in from other members of the team on the design of the interface. If the creative group cannot convince the team that their approach to the problem is right, this presents a cause for pause and further consideration. This is true for all deliverables. Dane believes for example, "if the navigation is confusing, then say so." These variables and others, make it impossible to say that one role is more important than another.

Chapter III: Supply and Demand

Demand for Artists and Designers in New Media

The demand for digital artist and designers varies from one office to another. The demand is generally high, because all development firms require digital designers to effectively build a website. In Atlanta, graphic designers are the digital artists who are in great demand, and it can take up to nine months to assemble a group of top notch designers for a team, according to Matis. She reasons,

> *"the supply is so short and the competition is tough. You walk out as a graphic designer; if you've done one website effectively, every company wants you. That's just how it is. Yes, they're feeling really good about themselves."*

As an IT job site, Computer.com has access to a database of creatives providing easy access. McDermott maintains that people use it as a tool, really like it, and see the site itself also has jobs. So finding people is not so much of an issue for these sites. It is just a matter the right jobs for the right people, and matching them correctly, because there are an extremely high number of new media positions on the site.

Like Matis, Hoover sees the demand for strong digital artists and designers as great. The dilemma is the difference between newly graduated creatives armed with the basic fundamentals, and those who are at the art director level. Senior level designers are very hard to find. These designers are great at what they do, and are ready to take their game to the next level as directors. The biggest challenge from Hoover's perspective, is what he thinks is also the case at other firms and agencies:

> *"We don't have a problem finding graphic designers to interview. We have a problem finding great graphic designers to hire."*

Dane sees the demand as "Very great." She concedes her designers are very busy and often work late hours, but believes this is partly due to their own passion and dedication. They also have the desire to make their clients happy, and for doing things they enjoy and are proud of. "Simply working hard does not reflect demand, because I think they would work as hard in any situation," says Dane.

Finding Qualified Artists and Designers

Many will agree there is a significant demand for creatives who can balance the both aesthetic and technical issues well. As Hoover and Matis lamented, the problem is finding excellent artists and designers to fill positions.

The exception again would be IT sites whose business it is to match people with positions. Processes and databases are in place and the pool of candidates is huge. They have free and easy access to databases generated as a normal part of their business. This also makes them first to review the candidates, and enables them to interview and make offers to the cream of the crop. On the other hand says McDermott, "we have a lot of clients coming to us who are just saying, please find these people for us. I don't have time to screen through hundreds of resumes."

Hoover believes the challenge in finding good creatives depends on the economy, saying "definitely, it's always been a tight market to find good people. Now, with the economy being what it is, it's twice as hard." His other point was the difficulty with finding creatives with new media skills which he describes as "three times as hard." This is because there are fewer creatives, and an ever-expanding market. Hoover describes the creatives with aesthetic and technical sensibilities as the "solid" artists and designers," and are the ones who are hard to find.

As a senior designer and applicant reviewer, Dane pointed out the same issue, and finds that creative services is always recruiting, "because it is very hard to find talented people who understand the traditional design skills, and also have new media skills." She finds that people are very much excited about the tools, and go to school to concentrate on the use of tools. As a result, they lack "traditional design skills, i.e. visual balance, typography, contrast, etc.

When reviewing portfolios, Dane takes a critical look at typography; an essential element of good visual communication. She also finds the same problem in reverse. These are designers who come in with a traditional design degree, but don't understand the new technology. Whether they lack aesthetic or technical skills, the assumption with both camps is, "I can learn that on the job."

However, according to Dane, the problem with both groups is most firms "do not have a separate group in place to train them;" this type of applicant has been a trend for many years. Dane observed,

> *"It's not that we don't have the time, it's just that we're not set up to do that kind of training and they don't have time to train on the job. As soon as someone is working on a project here, they need to be doing layout, they need to be creating the files. They need to understand how the whole system works."*

New Media Artists and Designers: Deficiencies

Matis has personally observed deficiencies in newly developed educational programs that were created to simply teach "new" things. Her example was a nephew who is in school majoring in Internet development. "He's literally majoring in how to build a website from start to finish, which makes no sense." Yet, "that's the way our educational system is progressing, she says."

She also lamented the fact that new graduates tend to be really good at one aspect of something stating, "either they're really strong client-side coders, or they make really pretty pictures." In either case, the problem is the fact that they tend to have no history or foundation in traditional design. Matis added,

> *"Where as, those of us who have more of a fine arts background, started with the wheel and worked our way forward. We have a more well-rounded skill set and a different view of things."*

Again, Matis also blames supply and demand, and academe's mandate to "crank people out" to meet market requirements. She compares it to going from kindergarten to sixth grade without going through the rudimentary steps of first through fifth, as one would normally take in the first years of formal education. In order to work through these deficiencies it requires additional mentoring and tutoring on the part of the employer which some may provide and others not. Matis believes the fundamentals are going to be missing until supply and demand become more balanced in the industry.

On the other hand, McDermott views the problem as a matter of figuring out what the employer needs in a candidate. Obviously, an entry or junior-level artist might not be great at everything. An employer has to say, "what am I going to build my team around?" At the entry level, you know they can eventually be trained in additional skills.

McDermott thinks one thing that feeds deficiencies in artists and designers is the fact that the computer programs change so rapidly in the field, making it hard to keep pace. Another is that some artists will marry themselves to an early version of the software, and become stuck.

For McDermott, deficiencies seem to be more of a fact of life in new media. Her perspective seems to be based on the candidate's attitude toward learning and change. The candidate should be able show an understanding of design concepts and processes, and a certain level of technical understanding. Still the candidate might may not have everything the company needs. She looks for candidates who can prove they can learn, have an interest and strong desire to learn more, and have the ability to change. She seeks out this potential in junior-level candidates, and believes at this level, "ability" [or potential] is more important than actual skills under the belt." She sums it up this way.

> *"If you have 70-80% of what we need, and 200% will power to learn the rest, then you are a desirable candidate. Flexibility is also desirable."*

In hiring candidates, McDermott wants to ensure that people have flexibility, potential, and passion for the work. These attributes are just as important as a candidate's skill set. What she does not like to hear is, "I am expert at one thing." She looks for signs of the their ability and desire to learn, and evidence that there is no stagnation in the candidate's outlook on a career in the industry. In an interview, she likes to hear the candidate say,

> *"I learn software quickly. I can just pick up a book and learn it, and I am not tied to any one technology. I've used this; I've used that. I can use whatever media you throw at me. Just give me the book, and I can play with it and learn it."*

Hoover acknowledges the great art schools in Atlanta, Pasadena, and elsewhere, and their strong focus on conceptualization, visual aesthetics, and design elements and principles. However, he finds difficulties on the technological and analytical side. He noted deficiencies in their ability to work with the tools that are currently available, coupled with the struggle to keep pace with the changing technologies. In many instances Hoover finds newly graduated candidates often have attended schools that have not provided them with the opportunity to work with any digital tools but basic creative skills only. He laments, "that's probably the biggest pain right there."

Unlike Hoover, Dane does not think it is a problem with the schools that are teaching the traditional design skills. Instead, she thinks it is the huge mass of people who want to get into the new media industry who seek to use the new tools creatively, not realizing they still need an art or design foundation.

Dane has found this to be a problem at other firms where she has worked as well. This is the issue of artistic skills versus technological know how. Though she admits the solution is not clear, she prefers universities with masters programs that will teach new media skills to someone who has the traditional skills in an established discipline such as graphic design, industrial design, animation, journalism, etc. Dane sees the attributes of these disciplines as being difficult concepts to convey before one has been taught what they are. Essentially, the rudiments of the discipline should become the foundation upon which other skills are added.

A need for strong communication skills is also a must according to Dane. A creative should be able to stand up in front of a client and describe and support the concept she/he is proposing, and/or ask questions that are going to help them reach the goal of solving the problem. So often artists and designers focus on the visual, but the ability to verbally express thoughts and ideas coherently is also helpful.

Additionally, Dane thinks someone with visual art skills should be involved in recruiting candidates for firms, so that undesirable candidates can be screened out before being sent out on an interview. A few projects and a resume listing software do not give enough information to select a candidate to send out to a firm. The recruiter must also be able to recognize good design in the work being presented. Yet typically, recruiters do not have the necessary visual design skills.

Here is a list of the deficiencies the participants found most frequently in new media artist and designers:

- Lack of Foundational Visual Art and Design Concepts (the Discipline)
- Lack of Knowledge of Art and Design History (the Development of the Discipline)
- Lack of Knowledge of New Media Technologies
- Inability to Keep Pace with New Media Technologies
- Lack of Communication and Presentation Skills
- Lack of Access to New Media Tools

The Visual Elements and Organizing Principles of Design

One of the most desirable, yet often missing skills observed industry leaders in new media art and design, is the lack of core design knowledge among new media creatives namely, the visual elements and organizing principles of design and how to apply them. How important is this core knowledge? Well, they are the tools and language of art and design. At the foundation of every degreed artist and designer's education, is knowledge of the visual elements and organizing principles of design.

In fact, artists and designers of all types use them, whether they are painters, sculptors, ceramicists, crafts people; or architects, graphic designers, illustrators, industrial designers, landscape designers, fashion designers, etc. Wong (1993) agrees noting, "in the first year's curriculum of every art school or university art department, regardless of the fields of specialization the students are to follow later, there is always a course variously called Basic Design, Fundamental Design, Two-Dimensional Design, etc., which deals with the grammar of this visual language."

All forms of visual art, over the millennia and throughout the world are marked with the character of these elements and the way they are organized. These visual elements and organizing principles determine what the work of art will be like (Gilbert, 1998). New media creatives who work in the area of new and emerging media, should be aware of these elements and principles which also transfer to the new genres made available through digital technologies.

The following are lists that define the elements and principles of design:

The Visual Elements:

Line (actual, implied, and formed by edges): A path made by a moving point.

Shape (geometric and organic): A two-dimension area with identifiable boundaries.

Form [Shape or Mass], (geometric and organic): A three-dimension area with identifiable boundaries.

Texture *(actual, visual, and pattern):* the feel and appearance of the surface; surface quality.

Lighting *(actual and the illusion of light):* The way the subject is lit.

Value *(high key and low key):* The relative lightness or darkness of a hue

Color *(natural, applied, local, impressionistic, and interpretive):* The property of objects that depends on the light they reflect.

Space *(two-dimensional and three-dimensional):* Gives definition to other elements of art.

Time *(elapsed time, viewing time, time as the subject, and change through time):* A limited period during which an action, process, or condition takes place.

Motion *(actual and the illusion of motion):* A movement, action or gesture.

Form *(shape or mass):* Geometric and Organic, A three-dimensional area with identifiable boundaries.

The Organizing Principles:

Unity *(compositional):* A sense of things visually belonging together.

Repetition*:* A repeated design element.

Variety: Change rather than sameness through space and time.

Balance *(symmetrical, asymmetrical and radial):* Stability of visual weight

Emphasis *(by location, or through drama, light, shape and/or contrast; subdued emphasis):* Viewer's attention centered more on certain parts of a composition than others.

Focal Point: A specific spot to which one's attention is directed.

Proportion: Size relationships between parts of a whole.

Scale: Size in relation to some constant or "normal" size.

Rhythm *(metric, flowing, swirling and climactic):* A pattern of elements suggesting movement, or pace in a work of art.

Economy *(economy of means):* To pair away all extraneous details.

Relationship to the Environment: The relationship of a piece to its intended environment.

Salary Ranges

I am always amazed at how people shy away from discussing money issues. After all, it is part of the reason there has been such a huge interest in new media careers over the past five years. It is also a topic on most people's mind throughout their careers, whether its new media or old media. Though none of the participants interviewed were from the human resource area, some gave ranges instead of specifics.

Matis suggested the range for a graphic designer's salary "can go anyone from an entry level of about $28k per year, all the way up to about $90k for a very senior person." This senior designer is that individual with multiple years of experience who started in print communications, then transitioned into the Web with a full history within design for the Internet.

Employers tend to advertise lower numbers than the actual jobs are paying, observed McDermott. Accuracy depends on who actually filled out the survey and their level. She noted that the people who make higher salaries tend not to take the time and fill out the salary surveys. Also, what employers say they pay, is usually significantly higher that what Computer.com salary surveys shows.

Sites like Computerjobs.com regularly conduct salary surveys, and McDermott has found many candidates respond saying, "your salary survey was low." She thinks the actual salaries people are getting varies, and is greater than what they are recording on surveys. She also finds gender discrepancies in the surveys finding that men really do make more money than women. She attributes this in part, to the fact that women tend to drop out of the work force more frequently, and can't get back in at the previous salary.

"It's also regional," she notes. An artists can expect more money working in Silicon Valley than in Atlanta. It's also based upon what kind of skills you have. For example, if you have programming (or authoring skills as a graphic designer, you can command more. So, the level of experience, what you have done, and what you're able to show you have done, all can and do come in to play. Someone who is just following directions may not command much of a salary. However, if you can show creativity, leadership abilities, and strong previous results, then you will be perceived as one who adds great value and will be compensated accordingly. McDermott explains further:

"If you are maintaining and retaining that talent, managing a whole department of graphic designers, you can expect more. If you can come in and show that you can assemble and retain talent, and you have the talent to work with and lead that team to create some of the best ad campaigns for major entities, then your salary will reflect this. I would think that would definitely create a six-figure salary. A lot of it is based on what you can produce."

In terms of entry-level positions, during the recession of 1991, McDermott was in her first position hiring graphic designers, they were hired in the $15k – $19k range. So, only about eight to ten years ago, starting out with a salary in the high teens was the norm. Now she is seeing starting salaries at around $35 – $45k for entry-level designers; this is a significant increase.

Dane could not comment on salaries. Though this information was proprietary for Hoover; he did not feel comfortable giving out specifics, but did give estimates saying, "it all depends on the type of firm you are in."

"I will tell you that it probably ranges anywhere from $42,000 to $120,000. Forty thousand might be the low-end for someone just coming out of school. I've seen people from the creative director's standpoint, paid $200,000 a year; so that's possible."

AIGA | Aquent Survey of Design Salaries 2001

Position	Salary/Wages	Total Compensation	Number Responding
	25th% median 75th%	25th% median 75th%	
Owner, Partner, Principal	$60k, $84k, $125k	70k, 1000k	156k, 905
Creative /Design Director	$60k, $77.5k, $100k	62.4k, 84k	115.5k, 846
Art Director	$45k, $58.8k, $72k	48k, 62.5k	80k, 1,424
Senior Designer	$43k$50k$60k	45k54k	65k, 1,751
Designer	$34k, $40k, $45.1k	35k, 40k	49,900, 2,130
Entry-Level Designer	$25k, $30k, $35.1k	27k, 31k	38k, 871
Solo Designer	$40k, $58k, $75k	44k, 60k	80k, 461
Print Production Artist	$30k, $36k, $43k	30k, 38k	45k, 565
Print Production Manager	$38k, $45k, $55k	39.8k, 48k	59,800, 445
Copywriter	$38k, $45k, $58k	40k, 50k	63.5k, 489
Web Designer	$40k, $50k, $60k	41.5k, 52k	65k, 566
Web Developer	$42k, $50k, $65k	44k, 55k	75k, 329
Web Programmer	$47.5k, $60k, $75k	48.7k, 65k	85k, 204
Web Producer	$50k, $61.5k, $80k	50k, 69k	85k, 190
Content Developer	$36k, $43.5k, $60k	36k, 47.5k	62.5k, 94

2000 Compensation, National Overview
Source: American Institute of Graphic Arts, NY

Corporate Culture

Today, we hear so much about the "corporate culture" that exists within the new media workplace and how it varies from one company to another. Matis observed a team-oriented, family-type environment. She noted, "we all know each other's spouse's names, as well as those of the children, and pets. We work together, and play together."

Matis believes when in a position where jobs and the resources are available, the individual looking to be hired really has such an upper hand. She explains,

> *"It comes right down to is asking, 'What kind of environment do I want to work in. Do I want the cool, the hip, or the chic? Do I want the cool, hip, chic, and family? Do I want the IBM blue box? What do I want?' [Then,] gravitate towards what you like."*

McDermott described a playful, casual atmosphere that included such items as a pool table, a dartboard, video games such as Hubert™, Tempest™, and Ms. PacMan™, and several other old 80's video games in the break room. These are free for employees to play. McDermott reflects,

> *"I remember once I was having a really stressful day with one of my staff members. So, I said, "come here, we need to meet in the break room—OK, a game of Ms. PacMan™, now." So, it's really relaxed."*

The firm also sponsors a two company baseball teams, and each June they have employee appreciation week, marked by a series of activities. Each month the company comes up with something special like taking the whole group to a nice restaurant, or a rock climbing expedition. These activities are instituted to promote team building, camaraderie, collaboration, and maintain high morale. McDermott said,

> *"I think that's the reason why I chose this company, and why I really like being here. It's the camaraderie. We find it important that you work hard, as well as play hard."*

45

It is also good business, and is done to attract highly skilled creatives. McDermott wants to attract people who would enjoy a fun and casual environment. It also realizes that when the job market is strong, they can walk out and readily find another position.

> *"Also, you have to be the right fit for our culture. If you're not the right fit, we're not going to be happy. I've interviewed some people and we have discussed our culture; and what they seemed to want was more of a corporate, structured environment—a bit more stuffiness."*

McDermott also recommends a good sense of humor, especially with the stress of deadlines, competition, etc. She believes that stress to be a good thing, because it can lead to growth when managed properly.

Hoover spoke of an environment that is smart and driven, "not driven to be the biggest company, but to be the best." He thinks many firms only lead you to believe they are the best, and have everything figured out. He says, "I would run from anyone who says they do." The Sapient culture from Hoover's perspective, is built on growth and constant change. He believes the day the firm "stops changing is probably the day many people here are going to walk out of the door."

He also concedes the culture is one of fun. Also, the people at Sapient, fundamentally believe the firm produces great work. They have developed a "One Team" approach that involves a process involving Discovery, Definition, Concept, Design and Implementation. It requires collaboration, and teamwork with groups on the team.

There is also an element of fun in the environment which supports understanding and collaboration. I could not help but notice two employees playing table tennis on a full-sized ping pong table as I entered the creative services group workspace at Sapient.

The culture in Dane's workplace is very much about passion. They want people to be keenly involved in what they do. For that reason, there is a have a lot of flexibility in the actual role that one has. Dane noticed this when she first joined the firm, how they were open to not putting her into a specific role. They wanted to hear what she was passionate about first; then, she was placed in the role.

In terms of internal activities and distraction, Dane believes it also reflects a part of that passion which basically says, *"we expect people to work very hard, so we expect them to play hard as well." They have foozball and pool tables, Sony™ PlayStations™, etc."*

There are scheduled breaks as well. For example, they might order in a Ben and Jerry's ice cream break. On the other hand, if someone is working hard, and does not want to break from their project, it is not a problem. They can pass on playing or scheduled breaks, until another time.

Also, parties are planned several times a year. These often include a stage and a couple of local or regional bands. An open bar, and dancing might also be involved.

Dane spoke of open house events two or three times each year. These are times to invite the clients, community, universities, and recruiters in to see the facilities, ask questions of different departments, see new projects on display, and experience demos. These have also proved to be good networking events for the firm. The open house events are open to the public. Other events are targeted to specific groups, and may involve dinner with clients, or something aimed at new recruits. Both kinds of engagements are important to the culture and life of the company.

Chapter IV: Knowledge and Skill Set Requirements

On the Job Training

With the deficiencies in skills among digital design workers discussed earlier, it's important to know what types of training firms are willing to provide on the on-the-job basis. Matis sees the new media workplace as a learning environment with the "desire to learn" as a prerequisite. Her workplace offers learning opportunities for employees from the most senior general manager, to the junior most individual. Learning opportunities within the digital design group may take the form of seminars where a company person will pick a topic and spend three hours teaching it, or a one-on-one mentoring session between senior-level designers and more junior-level designers. There are also employee education programs that allow and worker to go outside of the firm to take classes. After an outside course or workshop, employees are expected to use and share the information.

The same sort of training is available at Computejobs.com where there is a generous budget for external training. However, it is spent on technical training, versus artistic theory and practice. They only hire people who already have the background or foundation in design fundamentals, conceptualization, etc. McDermott says, "you want people with a strong foundation." She does not want to bring people in to establish a foundation of design concepts, but would much rather spend the money on technical skills for someone who has the basics.

According to Hoover, Sapient also embraces learning with respect to technology for its creatives; it aims at keeping pace with emerging technologies and prides itself on keeping people in the know. With the fast paced changes in new media, the firm feels "forced to move very quickly, and have to embrace learning," said Hoover.

Sapient also gets people trained through internal and external channels. Training can take the form of approaching new tools through an outside source, where an employee would take a course and bring the information back in-house. However, much of the growth gained in the design group is gained through employee interaction. Creative directors or design directors mentor the junior-level designers as part of their job responsibility. Newly graduated artists and designers perform work that is very important to the firm. Yet, it is the people they are going to work with from a mentoring standpoint who can assist most in their growth and development.

In Dane's environment, the mentoring approach to growth is also evident. Through a hierarchy within the creative services group, a new designer is placed on a project with a more senior-level designer. The idea is not to "just throw them on a project alone, at the beginning.

Another mentoring method involves peer reviews where the creative directors will get together to discuss the progress of different designers in the department. It is not a judgmental discussion, for example, ranking them on a scale of one to ten. Rather, it is more a discussion of where their strengths and weaknesses are. As a result of these discussions, they are better able to pair junior-level creatives on projects with senior people who will help them reach the goals they want to achieve. Dane added,

> *"This allows them to do what they are good at, or to do the things that they would like to learn to do by pairing them with someone in that area with that skill."*

Additionally, Dane's group will only hire people who have a high level of aesthetic sensibility and artistic skill. However, if they notice an individual is leaning more in a certain direction on projects, or the director feels they have gotten into the rut of using certain techniques over and over again, they are allowed to rejuvenate. They are allowed to step back and take a course in the area in question, even if it is a creative course they have had before. The real purpose is to review everyone's work, and try to bring them up to the level they want to be.

They might also pay for outside training for the acquisition of these skills. For example, they have had designers in the creative services area take outside courses in typography, color theory, while Web authors have taken Dreamweaver™ and other Macromedia™ courses. Creative directors here have taken business courses. Dane concedes,

> *"anything that we think they need to achieve the skills to move to the next level. I think to view yourself as*

> *someone who has complete knowledge of any one area is somewhat pretentious."*

Additional courses also provide knew knowledge that can be applied directly to projects. For senior-level individuals, they also illustrate new ways professors are delivering the courses and explaining concepts. It is helpful, as a creative director mentoring junior-level creatives, to have knowledge of new teaching methodologies in order to reiterate it to other people. Dane admits,

> *"As a creative director, I need to be a mentor and teach other people. If I take a course, even in something I already know; it will help me to better teach people."*

Temperament and Personality

Any creative job requires a depth and breadth of skills and emotions. However, Matis believes success for creatives is not as simple as "these are the skills and personality traits you need to succeed." A designer's temperament and personality, from her perspective, might be introspective, preferring to work singly, while others may be extroverted and totally out front, preferring the dynamics of group interaction. Both types have and can become successful creatives.

> *"There's no formula. Success is something you desire and it's something that is made available to you. It's just a matter of whether you really want to achieve it or not."*

When considering a candidate for hire, McDermott tends to go with those who are flexible, have a sense of humor, and have a passion for learning. She thinks the ideal candidate should be even-tempered, and able to work well under pressure.

Additionally, she also looks for a positive attitude when interviewing a candidate and sees it as most important; the ability to believe they can overcome obstacles is vital. These attributes support the idea of being self-confident which is essential. Finally, McDermott observed,

"We look for solution finders or problem solver— people who see things as a challenge instead of a diversion."

At the top of Hoover's list are attributes such as passion for learning, open-mindedness, and intelligence. Not only should the successful candidate be and willing to readily share their knowledge, but able to receive knowledge from other people as well. Basically, he believes creatives should take pride in what they do, and be passionate about their work. Hoover says,

"They're not just putting out this thing because that's what they get paid to do. They put a lot of themselves into their work, and want to see it all the way through."

Finally, flexibility is important at Sapient where the creative group normally generates multiple solutions at the end of the concept development phase. When the three or four potential solutions are presented, for example, the client may or may not select the creative's favorite solution; this would require flexibility on the designer's part.

Technical Tools

The tools digital artist and designers use depends on which component of the project they develop media for. Matis' workplace the tool are varied and numerous. The developer tools used by design techs can range from hard code to html editors to hybrid programs. They might combine pure code with off the shelf applications.

On the other hand, rare's digital designers don't touch code. The tools they use are also varied. Matis believes an employee has to be comfortable in order to be productive and creative. The creative services group believes in providing the tools that the artist feels most comfortable using, instead of locking someone into a particular software program.

In terms of draw programs, both Adobe Illustrator™, and Macromedia Freehand™ are available, for example. The tools include those for image manipulation, type styling, drawing, page layout, Web optimization, file conversion, etc. Still the post-production group would have another set of tools such as Adobe After Effects™, and so forth. The tool will also vary from one firm to another.

The shear number of digital tools and the rapid pace with which they change is what makes a passion for learning essential. Also, methods for learning new media are important. In other words, a way by which artists can ramp up quickly on new development tools. Once the artist has a method for staking out a new product, the same system could be applied to learning new applications as they emerge repeatedly. According to Matis, this is what educators should teach. She admits,

> *"There's so much out there for all of us to learn. It's a matter of making available to us the methods for learning. If you teach us how to learn, we can learn anything."*

Like Matis, McDermott does not want her designers to program, or write code. Like Dane, she believes the reason for this is to "allow people to do the best at what they're most passionate about." Also, from the usability perspective, she wants them to create the best design, not necessarily what programmers "know" will work via the program. Dane does not want creatives to think or create like a programmer, because it causes them to loose their edge, forget who the user is, and start thinking like a programmer. In other words, they would start to design in a way that was most easily programmed. McDermott has observed this many times with designers saying,

> *"Once they start getting into programming, they'll pick certain select boxes or submit buttons. You'll put in submit buttons where they don't make sense, just because it's easier to call information from the database that way."*

They know it makes sense from a programmer's perspective. However, it doesn't make sense to the end user, to have three submit buttons on the screen, for example. So, McDermott thinks programming somewhat hinders designers. While she agrees with Hoover that having a diverse skill set makes creatives more marketable, saying "people hiring like to see lots of skills." However, it does not allow designers to do the best at what they're most passionate about.

Instead, McDermott wants them to be user interface designers, and never lose site of user needs and desires. She believes if they become heavily involved in programming, they would tend to work within the constraints of what the programming language could do on the back end.

> *"I want the programmers to program, because it's the right thing to do for the user. I want the programmers to struggle to figure out the way to make the correct user interface work."*

The standard tools for artist and designers according to Hoover include Photoshop™, Illustrator™, Dreamweaver™, Flash™, etc. Dane, on the other hand, has digital painters on her team, and they paint on the computer infusing a combination of traditional and new media tools. Traditional tools (pencil, paper, ink, etc.) are still employed by creatives. They are then scanned or digitized for further development on the computer.

Within Dane's studio, traditional tools are also used for storyboarding, animation, video, and screen design. This work is typically done with sketchbooks, markers, etc. It could also be done on digital whiteboards that allow for the capture and saving of ideas digitally.

So they use a mix of hand-rendered sketching with the newest digital tools, though most of the work is done on the computer. The software applications include Adobe™ Illustrator™, Photoshop™, Pagemaker™, and Freehand™; QuarkXpress™; Metacreations' Painter™; Microsoft's PowerPoint™, Excel™, and Word™, etc. On the interactive, animation and video side, Dane's group uses Visio™, Macromedia Dreamweaver™, Director™, Flash™; Adobe Golive™, Web Tracker™, Java Script, DHTML, 3D Studio Max™, Maya™, Avid™, Final Cut Pro™ editing tools, and defect-tracking programs.

Expected Work Hours

Matis contends that those who understand the new media arena, know that because it is project based, there will be certain weeks were an artist or designer might only have 10 to 15 hours of work to do. Then, there will be weeks where it's going to be an 80-hour week job. She says,

> *"We've chosen this lifestyle. So you can't definitely say it's on average, 60 hours a week and four hours*

> *mandatory on Saturday. You just can't—not in this industry."*

Conversely, Matis sees the choice as one artist and designers do not have to choose. Work can be found at traditional agencies where they might find a more typical nine to five scenario. With this choice also comes time after a project has rapped up. According to dane,

> *"all you are doing is documentation and going out to a pond in the back to go fishing. That's part of the reward for the hard work you put in."*

Or, this might be a time when "you get to not show up for a few days." This is the work lifestyle that Matis and other have chosen in full view of the working hours required.

Likewise, McDermott reports of the ebb and flow of work which causes variance in the creative's work week. A week in which they are coming out with a new product, or doing the first round of prototypes, it might be a 50 to 60 hour week.

However, they try to be fair, realizing that people have families and lives, and they sometime have to "kick people out of here," says McDermott. But it's not a late night shop or sweatshop." McDermott thinks the hours are relatively fair and wants people to have balance. In fact, computerjob.com has instituted an incentive where the paid time off was increased, and everyone is encouraged to take it.

She contends that there are many forty hour weeks as well. Also they try to avoid weekend work altogether for creatives and management. According to McDermott,

> *"If the servers go down, for the IS department there might be. For client services people, perhaps. For us, very rarely are there non-tradition work hours."*

For Hoover's group, the average work-week is 53.5 hours. Again, at times, there is a steady stint of longer hours. Like the environments of Matis and McDermott, people work less than that at times. Also, they might also work more than 53.5 at times. Yes, they do. Again, it really depends on what phase of the project they are in.

On average, Dane's group tries to keep to a forty-hour week, so creatives can avoid burnout. Every weekend, there might be at least one creative in the studio. Some weekends there might be two or three people there. However, there are many weekends when artists and designers are not working.

Dane has observed that creatives will work late, and it is hard to tell if it is project work. For example, "sometimes people will stay there to do things to enhance their own personal skill set." Those who do work late, typically leave around eight p.m. However, a normal workday will run from "eight-thirty or nine o'clock a.m., to six-thirty or seven o'clock p.m." Dane observed also that the studio is pretty full from nine a.m. to seven p.m.

What are They Looking For?

Matis expects the entry-level candidate to look for the rudimentary portions of what they are going to be doing for them including aesthetic skills and knowledge of the standard programs for image manipulation, illustration, and layout, etc. She is also looking to see if they "have a comprehension of Web design." They are looking to see if this individual will work within the group's "family." To accomplish this, they require their creative services group to talk with the candidates.

> *"We've built a team here that's strong. Basically, we're married to each other, and have no choice in that. The individuals have to work together very closely."*

The group tries to establish a rapport with the candidate up front. This sort of relationship building continues as the new hire comes on board. Much of it seems to be the ability to get along with a variety of personalities and other differences in co-workers, and if not to understand, then to appreciate.

McDermott wants to see candidates demonstrate knowledge and analysis of their portfolio. She likes to see what see calls "real work" in order to prove the presence of a client, not just personal work. For an entry-level individual, this might be work completed as part of an internship, co-op education opportunity, or freelance projects.

The candidate should be able to speak of her/his meeting with clients, including client needs, the concepts proposed, etc. The creative should be able to say why a certain approach was taken. McDermott illustrates, in the case of a logo design and says,

> *"I didn't want to use any reds—so I used blues because they're conservative and the client is in the financial industry, so I wanted to make it clean. Or, it was an up-start ski business, so I used rash colors."*

Basically she wants to see strong conceptual skills and a needs analysis with evidence if their ability to design for an audience, and tie their design to the needs that were identified.

We want people to be creative, yet be able to work within parameters. She believes it is one thing to be creative, but if they did not follow any of the simple, brief guidelines given, it limits their effectiveness. So, the ability to follow directions is important. McDermott believes, "a good designer should be cognizant of the guidelines given, and infuse creativity within those specifications."

Hoover also looks to see if their work reflects an understanding of the basic fundamentals of design, in print and/or on-line media. He looks for not one, but a variety of styles when reviewing a designer's portfolio. He does not see the work environment as a clone type of space, but one where there are a myriad of personalities, and is less likely to judge people on what they are wearing.

Dane is watching for good communication skills and the way creatives present themselves. Like McDermott, she listens for how the creative talks about her/his work saying, "it's not just the work itself, it's how they feel about the work they are presenting." All of these things typically come through in the interview.

Additional Content and Concepts

The pressure is not only on designers to learn more beyond the core competencies, but for art and design education to offer more in order to better prepare creative new media professionals. Matis agrees the amount of information needed is great, and laments the schools offering quick six, twelve, or eighteen-month programs, that try to squeeze everything in. This would include certificate programs. These often fail according to Matis, in terms of art and design fundamentals most notably, but related history as well. These institutions must come to realize that students must "learn the basics" or the foundations of art and design as well. If they could find a way to incorporate these basics, she believes "the light bulb would go on."

Matis is fond of four and some two-year programs that have strong art and design curricula. However, she recommends design educators spend some time at new media firms. This would allow these educators to see how they work, think, create, and interact with each other, and use clients. She thinks there is still a chasm between academia and the real world. She noted,

> *"Maybe we need to cross over it and have you come play in our camp for a while. That way, you can see what our real world is, because in fact, you are training people to come into our real world."*

McDermott would like to see students prepared in a way that would allow them to take on other tasks if they choose, thereby growing into "what's best for them." From her perspective, it is important that they know what kind of career paths are available, what they are best suited for, and where they are headed. Also, the choice is theirs as to whether they want to continue as a graphic designer, get into illustration or 3-D art, or user interface design. They need to know if they want to be more of a creative director, or get into project management. Once they make the decision, they should be told it is possible, and the path should be communicated.

Hoover thinks educators should pay more attention to the development of the student's interpersonal skills, because they need to know how to interact in the team context. He believes experiences with and discussions about "group dynamics and collaborative processes would be helpful if properly infused into the curriculum. He agrees, the industry does change quickly, and sometimes schools cannot change as fast. However, he has seen some schools employ people from cutting-edge Internet development firms to team-teach or teach a class; "Georgia Tech has done this," Hoover says. This allows academe to hire people from industry who can bring the real world and the cutting edge experiences to the classroom. Hoover believes schools have to be dynamic.

Dane recommends educators include principles of good communications into the curriculum. She would also like to see creatives learn more about marketing in school. Currently, much of this is picked up on the job, though entering the firm with this knowledge, will put the creative at an advantage.

> *"It's not just about having a clean layout that looks good, but using color strategies and imagery in a*

> *certain way, and having styles that also communicate the same message."*

As a student, she did not think she would go into an advertising firm, so the topic did not interest her as much. However, she now realizes that understanding some of those concepts and methodologies for communicating messages is important. Dane believes supplemental courses or electives should include marketing and other business classes, along with communication courses that would include color theory as tool of communication.

While at Carnegie Mellon, Dane had an opportunity to take courses in the Art and Business track. This track dealt more with the business side of things, but she chose not to take any of these courses. Again in retrospect, she thinks some of them would have been of great benefit to her. She had to learn much of this information on the job, and thinks students should be encouraged to see a broader view of their discipline.

New Content, New Roles

As the art and design programs and course offerings evolve and expand to accommodate the current and future demands for these new media professionals, the roles a creative takes on may also evolve.

Matis projects more blurring of disciplines, and considers it positive and is excited about it. She recalls the start of the Web as we know it with the introduction of Mosaic™." Aesthetically, the Web was not visually appealing "because you had coders creating it" says Matis. The designers figured out a way to make the Web beautiful, information makes the Web intuitive and user friendly. She sees these three core disciplines merging more than ever in the future. She concedes that there will always be server-side technology specialists. However, the core builders: programmers, designers, information architects, Matis sees merging and becoming one unit.

> *"So, instead of having a design team and a technology team, I see that 23-year-old junior graphic designer at 30 [years old], able to do everything sitting at her home. That is, able to literally start-to-finish, build an e-commerce Web site."*

She feels similarly about video development and editing, saying it is "no longer going to be a specialty" discipline. Matis is excited because she envisions a day when it will be something we are all trained in, and understand how to do, just as we do typing today. Still, we might not all be good at it. There will always be specialists who concentrate on a particular technology. However, she sees the fundamentals or rudiments of the various related disciplines being a part of the core, as opposed to now where everything seems to be a definite specialty. "So, graying; we're looking forward to gray," says Matis.

McDermott sees creatives moving into other development disciplines related to the ones they started out in, yet she also sees them become team leaders, creative directors, managers, etc. What is really important to McDermott is for creatives to seek out and find their passion, or what they really want to do in the field. Then, "do it gusto."

Like Matis, Hoover, also purports more merging between disciplines. While a fundamental digital designer will always exist, he thinks we will begin to see some go into site development, where they use essential development tools such as XML, DHTML and Java Script, etc. He feels this makes them highly desirable and marketable. He believes most firms "will expect people to blend over into other areas because it is such a team-focused deliverable." It is vital that everyone understand the fundamentals of different areas, even if she/he is not working directly in it. Hoover forecasts,

> *"I think with technology especially, where we see the convergence of traditional and interactive media in technology, people who understand more aspects of technology, are going to have more doors open to them."*

Dane also thinks disciplines are going to evolve and combine more. She thinks we will increasingly need people with visual skills, i.e. the elements and principles of design and how to apply them. However, those with visual skills will have to learn more about motion, because of future increase in bandwidth (through-put) for the Internet. Interaction will not be limited to text and still images, but interactive motion and video content will become more of a demand. Information designers will need to begin to shape these areas as well. Dane thinks in the future, there is going to be more of a focus on the overlap in graphic design and filmmaking.

Brenda Smith Faison, Ph.D.

Advise to Academia

There is always much for educators and educational administrators to consider, and in light of new media; there is that much more. As educators plan for the education and training of the future generation of new media artists and designers, Matis advises educators to "listen to the children." She believes they know more about future trends than we ever will. While the toys we played with and figured out might have been analog, she contends, "You would be surprised at what these little kids are playing with and figuring out." She explains,

> *"It's like when I was a child, taking apart a toaster. Oh boy, that was the ultimate. These kids aren't just sitting there playing GameBoy™, they are analyzing GameBoy™, and in their heads they are building it! They are the future."*

Not only should educators listen, but ask questions of them, so as to build educational programs to meet their needs. Matis does not know if we as a community, nation, or world, will be able to pull programs together quickly enough to satisfy current and upcoming demands. She thinks educators should do the best they can with kids who are now nine to eighteen years old, and those currently in the job market. She contends,

> *"but build to the three to eight-year-olds, and what their future is going to be. Listen to them, and get ready for them."*

McDermott believes the future of some creatives is in software engineering, so academe should prepare for that. She contends that students should have the ability to question and know why they are developing the design. Students should also understand project management concepts, so they better understand the whole process. Dane has encountered designers who are very creative, but they don't know how to work within a business framework, and tend to want to work within a bubble.

> *"I actually had a graphic designer tell me in an interview, 'I just like to be left alone to do my work—*

> *to do my design, and I don't want any input,' which*
> *just really shocked me! I'm thinking, what are they*
> *teaching them in school."*

These new courses may currently be considered non-traditional in conventional art and design programs, but will become standard in future programs. McDermott also believes attention in these areas will give students a more well rounded skill set than previous generations.

As with Dane, Hoover believes students should be taught essentially how to learn or how to approach ever-changing knowledge, and help them to realize that learning is a life long process and they should be open to it. Educators should choose quality above quantity. He thinks some things will remain timeless, such as the fundamentals. Some learning takes place on the job, yet employers are less likely to pay for creatives to learn the fundamentals. Hoover would also like to see people walk away from school being able to say,

> *"I gathered the understanding and ability to learn,*
> *much better than I did before. I have the*
> *fundamentals, yet I am have been exposed to*
> *other things."*

Hoover also calls for educators to listen to students, and to be open and dynamic in the curriculum. Listen to what students are telling you, those are the people who know, for the most part. He reminds educators that it is not uncommon to see a thirteen-year-old carrying around a cell phone, or beeper.

> *"These young ones or kids have grown up with*
> *technologies, and they know a lot more about it than*
> *us. They are use to it. A lot of what they can tell us is*
> *where we need to go. So, open up your minds to*
> *the youth."*

He also believes that "the day of the lone genius is gone," and is a strong supporter of collaboration, group dynamics, and understanding the whole development process as academic content. Hoover declares,

> *"If history were to be rewritten, I think you'll find that in reality Michael Angelo had 13 or 14 other people working with him. The difference is in the way history was written then versus now. Now, you'd have the other members of the team mentioned, because it's actually more of a collaborative effort, both then and now."*

Dane strongly believes if someone has an understanding of the traditional design skills, and apply for a job somewhere, they may be told they need to know more about some of these technologies. However, if they learn quickly and pick up new media, they will fair better than someone who had the knowledge of the technologies, but no understanding of visual design. Her experience suggests it is harder to break them of bad design habits, and push them into traditional design concepts and skills.

She recalled the various conventional foundation exercises and admits, at the time she did not understand the point of the experimental lessons. They where developing skills involving the hands, the eye and the mind. An exercise might involve technologies as old as paper and scissors to create lines and shapes in the context of dynamic composition, good contrast, depth, balance, etc. However, Dane confesses,

> *"once you understand the purpose and value of those lessons, then all the new media is easy. It's like getting another new paint brush and you already know how to paint."*

Dane would have educators "stick to the basics." She recommends they continue to lay a strong art and design foundation. However, she does not write off the teaching of new media entirely saying,

> *"allow students to get a taste of what's out there. The educational arena might be their one big chance to gain access to technology. Once they graduate, they may not have the opportunity to get the equipment to learn the new media tools. So, it's nice to be able to learn the entry-level technology skills while in school; but the main focus should definitely be on teaching the traditional design concepts."*

Participants:
Interviewed: Spring 2000

Jackie Dane
Jackie Dane, at the time of the interview was Creative Services Director at iXL, Enterprizes, Inc. in Atlanta, Georgia. In November 2001, iXL merged with another industry leader, Scient Corporation. Scient is a results-oriented e-business, bringing together the "best of all disciplines, deep industry expertise, and proven solutions with eBusiness capabilities." It has positioned itself as an "Experience Management Consultancy," and is now focused on financial services, health and wellness, products and emerging opportunities industries. URL: http://www.ixl.com/index.jsp

Michael Hoover
Michael Hoover, at the time of the interview was Director of Creative Services at Sapient, Inc. in Atlanta, Georgia. Sapient is a leading business and technology consultancy which helps Global 2000 clients achieve explicit business outcomes through the rapid application and support of advanced information technology on a fixed-price basis. Founded in 1991, Sapient employs more than 1,900 people in offices in Atlanta, Cambridge (MA) Chicago, Dallas, Denver, Düsseldorf, Houston, London, Los Angeles, Milan, Munich, New Delhi, New York, San Francisco, Tokyo, Toronto and Washington, D.C. URL: http://www.sapient.com/default.htm

Eileen Matis
Eileen Matis, at the time of the interview was Creative Consultant at Rare Medium, Inc. in Alpharetta, Georgia. Rare Medium was an Internet professional services business and an international leader in Web design and development. On October 26, 2001, Rare Medium Group, Inc. announced that its subsidiary, Rare Medium, Inc., had completed the sale of its remaining Internet professional services business and certain related assets. URL: http://www.raremedium.com/

Cathy McDermott
Cathy McDermott, at the time of the interview was Creative Consultant at Computer Jobs.com in Atlanta, GA. ComputerJobs.com offers computer jobs and career management resources for technology professionals. ComputerJobs.com is the Internet's leading IT employment Web site. Founded in 1995 by and for information

technology professionals, the company provides its visitors with high quality computer-related job opportunities and career-related content organized into 18 vertical skill sets and 19+ major metropolitan markets.

URL: http://www.computerjobs.com/homepage.asp

Appendix 1: New Media Schools

New Media Centers

New Media Centers (NMC) is a non-profit organization that brings forward-thinking colleges and universities together with innovative high-tech companies to explore new ways of teaching and learning through new media. Founded in 1993, NMC has grown to include more than 100 educational institutions, connecting them to the resources they need to develop new media centers in their libraries, computing centers, and various academic departments. With the help of our corporate members, these centers give faculty and students alike access to the immense potential of new media. As a result, members are able to devise and demonstrate solutions and technologies that can be used in a wide variety of educational settings. NMC also provides a variety of members-only forums where a community of innovators in academia can learn from each other about pedagogical, legal, and technological issues in new media. What is new media?

According to New Media Centers, the term is a moving target. It can be described as new technology, such as DVD, haptics, streaming video, wireless transmission and Internet 2. However, new media can also be described as new uses for existing technologies such as digital libraries, interactive story telling, and distance learning.

What is a New Media Center? A New Media Center is the place on academic campuses where new media is incorporated into teaching and learning. In some cases it is the place where the emerging field of new media is being developed. NMC enables its academic members to:

1. open doors to the best minds and products at top high-tech firms
2. incorporate new media into their existing curriculum
3. connect to a diverse community of people finding solutions to similar challenges
4. offer cutting-edge staff development to build and enhance programs within the emerging discipline of new media studies
5. prepare students for new media careers

As a conduit to some of the most technology-friendly colleges and universities in the nation, NMC gives its corporate members the opportunity to:

1. collaborate with academic leaders
2. build brand recognition
3. beta-test new technologies

National Association of Schools of Art and Design

The National Association of Schools of Art and Design (NASAD) is an organization of schools, colleges, and universities that offer art and design studies. NASAD was founded in 1944 and now has 236 institutional members. It established threshold standards for undergraduate and graduate degrees and other credentials. Institutional membership is obtained and continued through the peer-review process of accreditation. NASAD provides statistical information, professional development, and policy analysis services. It also makes available for purchase, many helpful publications, including a listing of accredited institutions.

Recommended New Media Schools

From these two sources, I have developed a list if pioneering colleges and universities that have been innovative and continue to lead the way in developing and offering academic programs that focus on emerging media with aesthetic, cultural, and technological sensibility. These institutions of higher education are either a New Media Centers institution, an accredited member of the National Association of Schools of Art and Design, or are affiliated with both organizations. They are as follows:

Academy of Art College (San Francisco, CA)
http://www.academyart.edu

The Academy of Art College is an independent arts college offering programs and course work designed to prepare students for successful careers in computer arts, graphic design, industrial design, motion pictures and television, and seven other art and design disciplines. The College is a National Association of Schools of Art and Design accredited institution.

Art Institute of Boston at Lesley University (MA)
http://www.aiboston.edu

The Art Institute of Boston at Lesley University is a professional college of visual arts, offering programs and course work designed to prepare students for careers as Web and Multimedia Designers, Animators, Graphic Designers, Illustrators, Photographers, and Exhibiting Artists. The Art Institute of Boston at Lesley University is a New Media Centers institution.

Atlanta College of Art (GA)
http://www.aca.edu

The Atlanta College of Art is an independent art and design college affiliated with the Woodruff Arts Center, Inc. It prepares students for careers in electronic arts including Video, Computer Art, Computer Graphics, as well as Graphic Design, Illustration, and 7 other art and design disciplines. The College is a National Association of Schools of Art and Design accredited institution.

Bowling Green State University (OH)
School of Art
http://www.bgsu.edu/departments/art/

The Computer Art Program is a component of the School of Art at Bowling Green State University that focuses on creative expression using digital technology. The School allows students to investigate aesthetic and perceptual possibilities as they engage in alternative art discourses, preparing them for careers in Computer Animation (2D and 3D), Digital Imaging, Interactive Multimedia, Graphic Design and 12 other art and design disciplines. The School is a National Association of Schools of Art and Design accredited institution.

California State University, Chico (CA)
The Department of Communication Design
http://www.csuchico.edu/cdes/overview.html
The Department of Communication Design at California State University, Chico is an information design and communication department in a state university. It prepares students for careers in Graphic Design, Graphic Arts, Media Arts, Information and Communications Systems, Broadcasting, Communication, Communication Design, Instructional Design, and Electronic Printing and Publishing. The University is a New Media Centers institution (http://www.csuchico.edu/tlp/).

California State University, Hayward (CA)
Multimedia Graduate Program
http://manray.csuhayward.edu/multimedia/intro.html
The Multimedia program at California State University, Hayward is a graduate studies program offered through the University's Extended & Continuing Education Program in a state-supported university. It prepares students for careers in Multimedia, Media Production, Research Methods, Aesthetics, and Team-based Dynamics. The University is a New Media Centers institution (http://imctwo.csuhayward.edu).

City College of New York (NY)
Robinson Center for Graphic Arts and Communication Design
http://www.ccny.cuny.edu/electronic_design/
The Robinson Center for Graphic Arts and Communication Design is an art department within the College of Liberal Arts & Sciences within the City College of New York. It prepares students for careers in Electronic Design, Multimedia, and Visual Communications. The College is a New Media Centers institution.

Corcoran College Art and Design (Washington, D.C)

http://www.corcoran.edu

Corcoran College of Art and Design is an independent college of art affiliated with the Corcoran Gallery of Art. It prepares students for careers in Computer Art, Digital Arts, Digital Media Design, Graphic Design, and 8 other art and design disciplines. The School is a National Association of Schools of Art and Design accredited institution.

Fachhochschule Vorarlberg (Austria)
InterMedia Communications Design
http://www.fh-vorarlberg.ac.at/eng/edu/

InterMedia Communications Design and Interactive Media (IM) program is a component within the Fachhochschule Vorarlberg. The IM program prepares students for careers in Information Media, Management, and Communication, with a strong focus on the design of Interactive Media and Communication Processes. The Fachhochschule also prepares students for professional careers in Business and Engineering for the global work world of tomorrow. The Fachhochschule Vorarlberg is a New Media Centers institution.

Georgia Institute of Technology (GA)
School of Literature, Communications, and Culture
http://www.lcc.gatech.edu/
The School of Literature, Communications, and Culture is a unit of the Ivan Alan College of the Liberal Arts at Georgia Tech, and is comprised of three tracks: Information Design and Technology (IDT); Science, Technology, and Culture (STAC); and Women, Science, and Technology (WST). Through these programs it prepares students for careers as Designers, Producers, and Critical Analysts in Education, Business, and Industry and a changing digital culture. Georgia Institute of Technology is a New Media Centers institution
(http://www.newmedia.gatech.edu)

Maine College of Art (ME)
http://www.meca.edu
Maine College of Art is an independent professional college of art and design. It prepares students for careers in New Media Design, Graphic Design, Photography, and 6 other art and design disciplines. The College is a National Association of Schools of Art and Design accredited institution.

Maryland Institute College of Art (MD)
http://www.mica.edu
Maryland Institute College of Art is an independent college of art and design. It prepares students for careers in Digital Design/Illustration, Photography and Digital Imaging, Graphic Design, Illustration, Photography, and 9 other art and design disciplines. The College is a National Association of Schools of Art and Design accredited institution.

Memphis College of Art (TN)
http://www.mca.edu
Memphis College of Art is a professional college of visual arts. It prepares students for careers in Computer Arts, Graphic Design, Illustration, and Photography (Design Arts); and Computer Arts, and Photography (Fine Arts); plus 5 other art and design disciplines. The College is a National Association of Schools of Art and Design accredited institution.

Minneapolis College of Art and Design (MN)
http://www.mcad.edu
Minneapolis College of Art and Design is an independent college of art and design. It prepares students for careers in Animation, Comic Art, Digital Media, Interactive Multimedia, Filmmaking, Graphic Design, Illustration, Photography, and 7 other art and design disciplines. The College is a National Association of Schools of Art and Design accredited institution.

Mississippi State University (MS)
Department of Fine Arts
The Department of Fine Arts is the art and design unit within the College of Arts and Sciences at Mississippi State University, a land grant, state university. It prepares students for careers in Animation and Multimedia (Electronic Visualization), graphic design, photography, and 5 other art and design disciplines. The Department is accredited through the National Association of Schools of Art and Design.

Montclair State University (NJ)
Department of Fine Arts
http://www.montclair.edu
The Department of Fine Arts is an art department at Montclair State University. It prepares students for careers in Multimedia, Filmmaking, Graphic Design, Illustration, Photography, and 7 other art and design disciplines. The Department is accredited through the National Association of Schools of Art and Design.

New Jersey City University (NJ)
Department of Art
http://www.njcu.edu
The Department of Art is a department of visual arts within the College of Arts and Science at New Jersey City University, a state university. The Department prepares students for careers in Media Arts, Computer Arts, Graphic Design, Illustration, Photography, and 8 other art and design disciplines. The Department is accredited through the National Association of Schools of Art and Design.

New York State College of Ceramics at Alfred University (NY)
New York State College of Ceramics is a school of art and design at a state-supported college in a university. The College prepares students

71

for careers in Electronic Integrated Art, Video Art, Graphic Design, Photography and 6 other art and design disciplines. The College is accredited through the National Association of Schools of Art and Design.

Northeastern University (MA)
Department of Art & Architecture
http://www.art.neu.edu/
    The Department of Art & Architecture is an art and design program within the College of Arts & Sciences at Northeastern University. The Department prepares students for careers in Animation, Multimedia, Graphic Design, and 3 other art and design disciplines. Northeastern University is a New Media Centers institution.
    http://www.edtech.neu.edu

The Ohio State University (OH)
The Advanced Computing Center for the Arts and Design
http://www.cgrg.ohio-state.edu/
    The Advanced Computing Center for the Arts and Design is a technology-focused art and design center within The Ohio State University. The Center prepares students for careers in Animation and Film, Multimedia, Computer Visualization, Special Effects and Computer Graphics, Digital Video and Haptics. The Ohio State University is a New Media Centers institution.

Otis College of Art and Design (CA)
http://www.otisart.edu
    Otis College of Art and Design is an independent art school. The College prepares students for careers in Digital Media, Toy Design, Graphic Design and Illustration, and 6 other art and design disciplines. The College is accredited through the National Association of Schools of Art and Design.

Parsons School of Design (NY)
http://www.parsons.edu
    Parsons is an independent college of art and design that was founded in 1896, and is a division of New School University. The School prepares students for careers in Multimedia, Animation, Visualization, Fashion and Textile Computing (Design and Technology); as well as Communication Design, Illustration, Photography, and 6 other art and design disciplines. The School is

accredited through the National Association of Schools of Art and Design, and New School University is a New Media
Centers institution

Pratt Institute (NY)
http://www.pratt.edu
Pratt Institute is a school of art and design in an independent institution. The Institute prepares students for careers in Digital Design and Interactive Media, Computer Graphics, Film and Video, Art Direction, Graphic Design, Package design, Illustration, Photography and 9 other art and design disciplines. The Institute is accredited through the National Association of Schools of Art
and Design.

Rensselaer Polytechnic Institute (NY)
http://www.emac.rpi.edu/
The Electronic Media, Arts, and Communication (EMAC) track is one of the Arts Department programs supported by the Intergrated Electronic Arts at Rensselaer (iEAR Studios) facilities on the campus of Rensselaer Polytechnic Institute. With the vital multidisciplinary education necessary for leadership in a rapidly transforming information society, the program prepares students leadership in a rapidly transforming information society. Rensselaer Polytechnic Institute is a New Media Centers institution

Rhode Island School of Design (RI)
http://www.risd.edu
Rhode Island School of Design is a co-educational college of art and design, founded in 1887. It prepares students for careers in Graphic and Interactive Communication, Film, Animation, Video, Graphic Design, Illustration, Industrial Design, Photography, and 11 other art and design disciplines. The Institute is accredited through the National Association of Schools of Art and Design.

Ringling School of Art and Design (FL)
http://www.ringling.edu/
Ringling School of Art and Design is an independent school of art and design. Ringling prepares students for careers in Computer Animation, Photography and Digital Imaging, Graphic and Interactive Communication, Illustration, and 3 other art and design disciplines. The School is accredited through the National Association of Schools of Art and Design.

Rochester Institute of Technology (NY)

College of Imaging Arts and Sciences

http://www.rit.edu/

The College of Imaging Arts and Sciences at the Rochester Institute of Technology comprises a School of Art, a School of Design, a School for American Crafts, a School of Film and Animation, and a School of Photographic Arts and Sciences, all within the College of Imaging Arts and Sciences of a comprehensive Institution. It prepares students for careers in Imaging Arts: Photography and Computer Animation, Graphic Design, Industrial Design, Illustration, Professional Photographic Illustration, Medical Illustration, Photojournalism, and 12 other art and design disciplines. The College is accredited through the National Association of Schools of Art and Design, and the Rochester Institute of Technology is a New Media Centers institution

Salem State College (MA)

Department of Art

http://www.salem.mass.edu

The Department of Art at Salem State College is a department of visual arts in a state-supported college. The Department prepares students for careers in Interactive Multimedia, Graphic Design, Photography, and 5 other art and design disciplines. The Department is accredited through the National Association of Schools of Art and Design.

Syracuse University (NY)

School of Art and Design

http://www.syracuse.edu

The School of Art and Design is a school of art and design in a college of visual and performing arts in a university setting. The School prepares students for careers in Computer Graphics, Art Photography, Art Photo Process, Art Video, Film, Graphic Design, Illustration, and 11 other art and design disciplines. The School is accredited through the National Association of Schools of Art and Design.

Savannah College of Art and Design (GA)

http://www.scad.edu/

Savannah College of Art and Design is an independent art school that is an International University for the Arts. The School prepares students for careers in Electronic Arts, Computer Arts, Film, Animation, and 14 other art and design disciplines. Savannah College of Art and Design is a New Media Centers institution.

School of the Museum of Fine Arts, Boston (MS)
http://www.smfa.edu

School of the Museum of Fine Arts, Boston is a an independent art school that is a division of the Museum of Fine Arts, Boston offering degree program in affiliation with Tufts University. The School prepares students for careers in Electronic Arts, Computer Arts, Film, Animation, Graphic Design, Illustration, Photography, and 12 other art and design disciplines. The School is accredited through the National Association of Schools of Art and Design.

School of Visual Arts (NY)
http://www.schoolofvisualarts.edu

The School of Visual Arts is an independent art college. It prepares students for careers in Film, Video, and Animation (Animation, Cinematography, Directing, Editing, and Screenwriting), Computer Art, Illustration, Cartooning, Photography, and 12 other art and design disciplines. The School of Visual Arts is accredited through the National Association of Schools of Art and Design.

State University of New York, Buffalo (NY)
Department of Art
http://www.art.buffalo.edu

The Department of Art at State University of New York, Buffalo is a department of art and a separate department if art history in a college of arts and sciences within a state-supported university. It prepares students for careers in Computer Art, Photography, Graphic Design, Illustration, and 4 other art and design disciplines. The Department is accredited through the National Association of Schools of Art and Design.

Truman State University (MO)
Department of Visual Arts: Visual Communications
http://finearts.truman.edu/art/html/viscom.html

The Visual Communications Program is an applied art and design unit within the Department of Visual Arts in a state-supported university. The Program prepares students for careers in Design For Print, Web and Multimedia Applications, and subsets Of Visual Communications including Illustration and Photography (Digital And

Traditional). Truman State University is a New Media Centers institution. http://nmc.truman.edu/NMClook

Temple University (PA)
Tyler School of Art
http://www.temple.edu/tyler
Tyler School of Art is a college of art in a state-related university. Tyler prepares students for careers in Graphic and Interactive Design, CAD-CAM, Photography, and 12 other art and design disciplines. The School is accredited through the National Association of Schools of Art and Design.

University of Arizona (AZ)
College of Fine Arts
http://www.arts.arizona.edu
The College of Fine Arts is an arts and design unit in a university setting. It prepares students for careers in Media Arts, Intermedia, Animation, Multimedia, Website Design, Visual Communication, as well as Art, Dance, Music, and Theatre Arts. The University of Arizona is a New Media Centers institution (http://www.arts.arizona.edu/treistman)

University of Art and Design, Helsinki (Finland)
The Media Lab
http://www.mlab.uiah.fi
The Media Lab provides education in new media design and production within the University of Industrial Arts Helsinki (UIAH). The Media Lab prepares students for careers in Interaction/Information Design, Digital Authoring, and New Media Management. The University of Art and Design, Helsinki is a New Media Centers institution.

University of California, Los Angeles (CA)
Department of Design | Media Arts
http://www.design.ucla.edu
Department of Design is a design unit within the design and media arts component of the UCLA School of the Arts and Architecture. The Department prepares students for careers in Visual Communication Design with an emphasis on Digital Media, balancing aesthetic sensibility with logical reasoning, formal theories with practical application, and contemporary thought with historical

perspective. The University of California, Los Angeles is a New Media Centers institution. http://www.oid.ucla.edu/nmc

University of Cincinnati (OH)
College of Design, Art, Architecture and Planning (DAAP)
http://www.daap.uc.edu
   The College of Design, Art, Architecture and Planning is a college of art and design in a state-supported university. DAAP prepares students for careers in Digital Design, Electronic Arts, Graphic Design, Industrial Design, Photography, and 13 other art and design disciplines. The College is accredited through the National Association of Schools of Art and Design.

University of Florida (FL)
School of Art and Art History
http://www.arts.ufl.edu/art
   School of Art and Art History at the University of Florida is a department of art and art history in the land-grant university. The School prepares students for careers in Electronic Intermedia, Graphic Design, Creative Photography, and 7 other art and design disciplines. The School is accredited through the National Association of Schools of Art and Design.

University of Hawaii (HI)
Electronics Arts
http://www.hawaii.edu/art/flash/flashmenu.html
   The Electronics Arts Program is a new media program with in the Department of Art at the University of Hawaii at Manoa. It encourages students to explore the relationships between Art, Culture and Technology within an Intermedia environment while emphasizing the Theoretical Context of Art to prepare students for careers in the Electronic Arts industry. The University of Hawaii is a New Media Centers institution
   (http://www.dmc.hawaii.edu).

University of Illinois, Chicago (IL)
School of Art and Design
   The School of Art and Design the University of Illinois, Chicago is a school of art and design in a state-supported, urban university. The School prepares students for careers in Electronic Visualization, Electronic Media, Film, Animation, Video, Photography, Graphic Design, Industrial Design, and 2 other art and design disciplines. The

School is accredited through the National Association of Schools of Art and Design.

University of Louisiana at Lafayette (LA)
College of the Arts
http://www.arts.usl.edu
    College of the Arts is a department of visual arts, and a school of architecture, in a college of the arts in a university. The College prepares students for careers in Computer Art and Animation, Industrial Design, Photography, and 7 other art and design disciplines. The School is accredited through the National Association of Schools of Art and Design.

University of Massachusetts, Dartmouth (MA)
College of Visual and Performing Arts
http://www.arts.usl.edu
    The College of Visual and Performing Arts at University of Massachusetts, Dartmouth is a college of visual and performing arts in a state-supported university. The College prepares students for careers in Electronic Media, Photographic/Electronic Imaging, Illustration, Graphic Design, Typography, Illustration, and 9 other art and design disciplines. The School is accredited through the National Association of Schools of Art and Design.

University of New Brunswick (Canada)
Multimedia Studies
http://www.unbf.ca/arts/MMS/menu.html
    Multimedia Studies is a new media program in the Faculty of Arts that also runs concurrent degree programs with the Faculties of Computer Science and Education, and a joint degree program with the Faculty of Science at the University of New Brunswick. The Multimedia Studies program prepares students for careers in Multimedia Management, Design, Animation, Sound and Video. The University of New Brunswick is a New Media Centers institution.
    http://www.unb.ca

University of Oregon (OR)
Multimedia Design Program
http://mmd.uoregon.edu
    The Multimedia Design Program is a unit within the Department of Art, a component of the School of Architecture and Allied Arts. Multimedia Design prepares students for careers in professional

digital media design and production. The University of Oregon is a New Media Centers institution

http://nmc.uoregon.edu

University of the Arts (PA)
Philadelphia College of Art and Design
The University of the Arts is a college of art and design in a university of visual arts, performing arts, and media and communications. The College prepares students for careers in Animation, Film/Animation, Film/Video, Graphic Design, Industrial Design, Illustration, Photography, and 12 other art and design disciplines. The College is accredited through the National Association of Schools of Art and Design, and a New Media Centers institution (http://www.uarts.net/).

University of Southern Colorado (CO)
Department of Art
Computer Animation and Digital Art is an area of concentration in the Department of Art at the University of Southern Colorado. The Program prepares students for careers in Animation, Digital Imaging, and Video, for the Web and CD, and is a curriculum in which courses are integrated within the art major. The University of Southern Colorado is a New Media Centers institution (http://www.uscolo.edu/itc/cnm.html).

University of Wisconsin, Stout (WI)
Department of Art and Design
http://uwstout.edu
The Department of Art and Design at the University of Wisconsin, Stout is a department of art and design in a state-supported university. The Department prepares students for careers in Multimedia, Graphic Design, Industrial Design, and 3 other art and design disciplines. The Department is accredited through the National Association of Schools of Art and Design.

Wellesley College (MA)
The Art Department
http://www.wellesley.edu/Art/index.html
The Multimedia Arts Program is within the Department of Art at Wellesley College. The Department and it programs prepare students for careers in Multimedia, Film, Video, and 3 other art and design disciplines. Wellesley College is a New Media Centers institution

(http://www.wellesley.edu/Knapp/mtc.html).

Youngstown State University (CT)
Department of Art
http://www.fpa.ysu.edu/art

The Department of Art at Youngstown State University is a department of art within the College of Fine and Performing Arts. The Department prepares students for careers in Art and Technology, Graphic Design, Photography and 6 other art and design disciplines. The Department is accredited through the National Association of Schools of Art and Design.

Appendix 2: Related Books

Interactive Media: General and Design

Preparing Web Graphics
by Lynda Weinman, Published by New Riders Publishing
A less expensive, smaller version of Designing Web Graphics. A detailed guide to creating graphics for web delivery, shares tips and techniques for fast and high-quality web graphics, and covers such topics as cross-platform issues, compression methods, and transparent GIFs.

Designing Web Graphics 2
by Lynda Weinman, Published by New Riders Publishing
Second edition of Designing Web Graphics. This full-color guide will teach you the most successful methods for designing and preparing graphics for the World Wide Web. Completely updated and expanded to include the latest on file formats, file sizes, compression methods, cross-platform web color, and browser-specific techniques, Designing Web Graphics.2 is the definitive graphics guide for all web publishers.

Coloring Web Graphics
by Lynda Weinman, Bruce Heavin, Published by New Riders
How to work with color and image file formats for web delivery.

Deconstructing Web Graphics
by Lynda Weinman, Published by New Riders
Teaches good web design practices by analyzing and reverse-engineering successful Web sites.

Multimedia Animation
by Clarence Lamb, Published By Sams
Hands-on tutorial in animation for multimedia.

Designing Web Animation; with CD-ROM
by Nicola Brown, Peter Chen, David Miller, Paul Van Eyk, Published by New Riders
Samples of Web animation techniques, information about the tools needed to create animated Web pages.

Universal Web Design
by Crystal Waters, published by New Riders

A guide to designing web sites to maximize accessibility. A resource and guide to creating design alternatives for the Web, this book will lead Web site designers through those elements that can be easily—and some, not so easily—altered or enhanced.

Designing Multimedia: A Visual Guide to Multimedia and Online Graphic Design
by Lisa Lopuck, Published by Peachpit Press

If you're interested in being part of the booming field of multimedia, this beautifully-illustrated volume shows you how. Its concept-to-product approach is highly visual: with stunning, full-color samples of actual multimedia projects. Title structure, user interface, software dynamics, and many other factors that affect design decisions are explained in detail.

Designing Interactive Websites
by Gong Szeto, Matthew Butterick, Jeanne McKirchy-Spencer, Published by Hayden Books

Webmasters want to know what they can do to keep people coming back. Designing Interactivity for the Web gives secrets for using the best interactive elements (personalized content, targeted marketing, games, chats, discussions, etc.). Clear step-by-step instructions show the best and simplest ways to create interactivity.

About Face: The Essentials of User Interface Design
by Alan Cooper, Published by IDG Books Worldwide Inc.

An excellent book for anyone who wants to understand why so much software is so poorly designed – and an even better book for anyone who wants to DO something about the problem. Must reading (and doing!) for programmers of any level.

Designing the User Interface: Strategies for Effective Human-Computer Interaction
by Ben Shneiderman, Published by Addison-Wesley Publishing Co.

Based on 20 years experience, Shneiderman offers readers practical techniques and guidelines for interface design. He also takes great care to discuss underlying issues and to support conclusions with empirical results. Interface designers, software engineers, and product managers will find this book an invaluable resource for creating systems that facilitate rapid learning and performance, yield low error rates, and generate high user satisfaction.

Inside Electronic Game Design

by Arnie Katz, Laurie Yates, Published by Prima Publications

Inside Electronic Game Design opens the secret world inhabited by designers of computer, multimedia, and video games. Leading game designers are spotlighted and give insights into the concepts and dynamics of game making. Would-be game designers will learn how to professionally pursue a career in this booming industry.

Writing for Multimedia: A Guide and Sourcebook for the Digital Writer

by Michael D. Korolenko, Published by Integrated Media Group

This is a comprehensive book detailing writing for entertainment, children, science fiction thrillers, documentaries, and assessment programs. It teaches the user to develop non-linear writing skills, instructs them in a variety of techniques, and describes a variety of tools and methods (such as storyboards, flip-books and computer prototypes).

Multimedia Scriptwriting Workshop

by Douglas Varchol, Published by Sybex

A hands-on tutorial that walks readers through the basics of writing from CD-ROM products, this book shows how it differs from traditional scriptwriting, with side-by-side examples of how what it is written is transformed to the computer screen. It also includes interviews with professional writers who have made the transition from traditional scriptwriting to excel in this medium.

Multimedia Producer's Bible: Managing Projects and Teams

by Ron Goldberg, Published by IDG Books Worldwide

his book maps the entire process of multimedia production geared toward anyone who makes or plans to make a living off multimedia. It discusses the appropriate tools to use for various projects and legal issues and intellectual property concerns that multimedia producers face. The CD includes Director demo, Authorware demo, PageMill demos, SiteMill demos, Quest demo and more.

Designing Interactive Digital Media

by Nicholas V. Iuppa, Published by Butterworth Heinemann

This book shows how to design interactive programs in an age when digital technology makes just about anything possible and examines the expanded capabilities of digital video for increasing interactivity. The CD-ROM shows numerous examples of programs and their applications.

Web Page Design: A Different Multimedia

by Mary E.S. Morris, Randy J. Hinrichs, Mary E. S. Morris, Published by Prentice Hall

Revealing the crucial differences between an ordinary Web page and an effective site, best-selling Internet author Mary E. S. Morris goes beyond the basics of web creation to show readers how to tackle the crucial problems of information overload at your Web site, getting lost in cyberspace, bandwidth constraints required to hold a user's attention, and more.

Designing Multimedia Environments for Children

by Allison Druin, Cynthia Solomon, Published by John Wiley & Sons John

Demonstrating how to create vibrant multimedia environments to enhance a child's educational and play experience, a multimedia guide includes a history of children's software and profiles of the latest technologies. (Intermediate).

The Web Design Wow! Book: Showcasing the Best of On-Screen Communication

by Jack Davis, Susan Merritt, Published by Peachpit Press

Like every Wow! title, this book is packed with award-winning, real-world examples of Web sites and CD-ROMS with the very best interfaces. Step-by-step explanations show designers the concepts behind creating clear and engaging interfaces. The cross-platform CD-ROM includes most of the projects covered in the book, along with demo versions of the leading multimedia tools from Adobe and Macromedia.

Emerging Multimedia Computer Communication Technologies

by Chwan-Hwa 'John' Wu, J. David Irwin, Published by Prentice Hall

Learn all about the basic technologies for information transfer and networking - the hardware and the software, along with compression standards and techniques for transmitting data most efficiently. Then find out about the networks that link us together, from your home telephone and cable TV to office-sized LANs to the World Wide Web. Finally, see how communications networks harness the power of multimedia computers to create new applications and enhance old ones. At the same time, discover how you can make the most of these capabilities.

Getting Started in Multimedia Design
by Gary Olsen, Published by North Light Books
This is a beginners guide to creating and designing for multimedia. Along with the book, the author also has a supporting website to further assist readers.

Interactivity by Design: Creating & Communicating With New Media
by Ray Kristof, Amy Satran, Published by Hayden Books
The book explores how to use Interactivity, one of the hottest topics in the computer design industry. It highlights professional quality, 4-color groundbreaking design techniques, and features Interactivity as a design application in multimedia, CD-ROM, On-line and other applications.

Managing Multimedia
by Elaine England, Andrew Finney, Published by Addison-Wesley Publishing Co.
Providing an invaluable guide for multimedia producers, this book covers every stage of the management process from initial client meeting to delivery of the finished product. It focuses on client liaison, administrative processes and procedures, analysis, documentation, schedules, budgeting, team management and management of the major

Interactive Media: Software & Programming

Macromedia Animation Studio
by Gary Chapman, Published by Random House, Incorporated
The ultimate book/CD package for learning desktop animation using Macromedia Director, MacroModel and other applications. The CD is loaded with a searchable Macromedia Director reference, animated, interactive tutorials and $300 worth of clip media. It also has test-drive Mac and Windows versions of Macromedia Director.

Direct Draw Programming; With CD-ROM
by Bret Timmins, Published by
Henry Holt & Company, Incorporated

Tutorials, sample code and the step-by-step construction of a working arcade-style game to show programmers how to get the most out of this radical new API for Windows 95.

The GIF Animator's Guide
by Sandra E. Eddy, Published by MIS

This full-color guide first teaches you the basics of creating and editing images, explaining file formats, transparencies, color selection, design principles, and other issues involved with creating an image that you want to animate. Then the author explains how to plan an animation (you focus, for example, on the first frame); choose the effects and techniques to produce the look you want; and insert your animation in an HTML document.

Tricks of the Game-Programming Gurus
by Andre Lamothe, John Ratcliff, Tyler, Denise Seminatore, Ken Allen, Published by Sams

Outlines the basic and advanced principles involved in creating interactive games, including flight simulators, three-dimensional walk-through games, and various multimedia utilities, with an accompanying CD that includes shareware games and commercial demos. (All Users).

Michael Abrash's Graphics Programming Black Book
by Michael Abrash, Published by The Coriolis Group

No one has done more to conquer the performance limitations of the PC than Michael Abrash, a software engineer for Microsoft. His complete works are contained in this massive volume, including everything he has written about performance coding and real-time graphics. The CD-ROM contains the entire text in Adobe Acrobat 3.0 format, allowing fast searches for specific facts.

Official Netscape Guide to Web Animation
by Mark L Chambers, Published by Ventana Press

If you'd like to learn how create a wide variety of GIF animations, check out this book. The author covers lots of ground, starting off by teaching you how to prepare your images for animation with Jasc's Paint Shop Pro, Adobe Photoshop, and Adobe PhotoDeluxe.

The CGI Book
by William E. Weinman, Published by New Riders

A comprehensive tutorial covers the basics of CGI and enables immediate script writing, continuing to more advanced topics including image maps, server push, e-mail, HTML, and database lookup.(Advanced).

Director Close-up: Interactivity & Animation, Versions 4 & 5
by Peter Vaughan,Tim Vaughan, Published by Wadsworth

General guide to using Director for interactive products, including animation, Lingo and integrating digital audio and video.

Web Animation for Dummies
by Cynthia L. Baron, Renee Lewinter, Published by IDG Books Worldwide

Web Animation For Dummies helps you weigh all the pros and cons of the various options of animation on the web — but more importantly, this book helps you get right to work creating exciting animated graphics that are sure to enliven your otherwise-static Web pages.

HTML: The Definitive Guide
Chuck Musciano, Bill Kennedy, Published By:O'Reilly & Associates

A complete guide to creating documents on the World Wide Web, this second edition describes basic syntax and semantics and goes on to show readers how to create beautiful, informative, and dynamic Web documents they'll be proud to display.

Javascript: The Definitive Guide
by David Flanagan, Published by O'Reilly & Associates

The ultimate Javascript resource book. This second edition of the definitive reference guide to JavaScript, the HTML extension that gives Web pages programming-language capabilities, covers JavaScript as it is used in Netscape 3.,0 and 2.0 and in Microsoft Internet Explorer.

Designing Animation for the Web
by Hayden Development Team, Published by Hayden

Technical information and design advice about which technology to use for which specific needs.

Lingo!: An Advanced Guide to Director's Scripting Language
by Tab Julius, Published by New Riders

An introduction to doing serious programming techniques in Lingo, Director's scripting language.

Lingo Sorcery: The Magic of Lists, Objects and Intelligent Agents
by Peter Small, Published by John Wiley & Sons

Introduction to applying Object-Oriented Programming techniques in Lingo. Assumes basic knowledge of Director.

CD-Morph! Explore Gryphon Software's Amazing Special Effects and Animation Software
by Patrick J. Burns, Published by Addison-Wesley Publishing Co.

A step-by-step tutorial on the basics of morphing and demonstration of advanced morphing techniques.

Web Animation Bible
by Kris Jamsa, Published by Jamsa Press

Each day designers are faced with a myriad of tools that let them animate Web sites-from animated GIFs to streaming video clips. The steps you must perform to add ActiveX objects, real audio, or search engines, are not complex when you know the secrets. Web Animation Bible is a full-color book that examines the creation and use of animated graphics, the use of ActiveX controls to play audio and video, and the use of ActiveX control and Java to manipulate images and text. The book's companion CD-ROM includes the image, audio, and video files the authors use to build their projects, as well as related ActiveX controls and Java applets.

Lingo and Shockwave Sourcebook
by Vineel Shah, John Musser, Published by John Wiley & Sons

An introduction to Lingo for non-programmer Director users ready to start developing more complicated projects.

Photoshop Magic
by Brendon Perkins, Hayden Books

Advanced level Photoshop tips, designed around solving particular design problems (creating a stained glass window, simulating rain, etc.).

Learning Perl

by Randall L. Schwartz, Randal L. Schwartz, Larry Wall, Published by O'Reilly & Associates

Learning Perl is ideal for system administrators, programmers, and anyone else wanting a down-to-earth introduction to this useful language. Written by a Perl trainer, the book's aim is to make a competent, hands-on Perl programmer out of the reader as quickly as possible. The book takes a step-by-step, hands-on tutorial approach and includes hundred of short code examples.

Exploring Java

by Patrick Niemeyer, Joshua Peck, Pat Niemeyer, Josh Peck, Published by O'Reilly & Associates

Exploring Java introduces the basics of Java, the hot new object-oriented programming language for networked applications. This book also shows users how to quickly get up to speed writing Java applets and other applications, including networking programs, content and protocol handlers, and security managers.

Black Art of Java Game Programming

by Joel Fan, Eric Ries, Calin Tenitchi, Published by Waite Group Press

This book covers techniques for creating multi-user games and environments over the World Wide Web by using Java's networking capabilities. This is one of the first books to cover these techniques. The Game Gallery section gives in-depth information on some of the hottest Java games around, describing the game, how it works, and how it utilizes the features of Java. The CD contains complete Java source and byte codes to the class libraries and games developed in the book.

Black Art of Macintosh Game Programming

by Kevin Tieskoetter, Published by Waite Group Press

Thanks to this clear guide, Macintosh game programmers no longer have to resort to deciphering PC game books and arduously converting their codes for the Mac. Users are taken step by step through the basics of graphics, with tips on how to take advantage of the Mac's operating system. Tieskoetter also shares his secrets for optimizing code to achieve the fastest possible speed and details techniques for performing freeform texture mapping.

Black Art of Windows Game Programming
by Eric R. Lyons, Published by Waite Group Press

This book was written for programmers who are new to Windows, but are comfortable with programming in general. It gives concrete examples of how WinG can increase performance under Windows, introducing all the basic concepts with practical hints, tips, and techniques. The CD-ROM contains the best of Microsoft's multimedia and game development tools.

Dynamic HTML in Action
by William J. Pardi, Eric M. Schurman, Published by Microsoft Press

Readers will learn how to create dynamic Web content using multimedia controls, Cascading Style Sheets, scripting languages, active channels, and Dynamic HTML. All topics are covered in clear, succinct language with plenty of samples on the CD-ROM to make learning these new tools as engaging and interesting as the content Web users will eventually create.

Hands on Cold Fusion 4.0
by Steve Griswold, L. Allan Austin, Abraham Lloyd, Robi Sen, Chris Severud, Published by Prima Publication

Cold Fusion allows developers with basic HTML skills to take their work to the next level. This book covers how to create Cold Fusion applications, which will teach readers about Cold Fusion while also letting them create useful applications that they can deploy in their Web sites.

Animation: Traditional

Breaking Into Film: Making Your Career Search a Blockbuster
by Kenna McHugh, Published by Petersons Guides

Independent film producer, writer, and public relations professional Kenna McHugh tells how to find an internship on a movie set—behind or in front of the camera—how to network, how to focus on an area of interest, and much more, in this unparalleled guide to breaking into the movie-making industry. Includes appendices of key employees.

Cartoon Animation Introduces the Basic Skills (Basic Skills)
by Walter Foster, Published by Walter Foster Publishing, Incorporated

Looking Inside Cartoon Animation
by Ron Schultz, Chris Brigman (Illustrator), Published by John Muir Publications

Using artwork from DIC Enterprises' popular Inspector Gadget cartoon series, this book illustrates how cartoons are brought to life. To produce one 30-minute animated film, four months and over 40,000 cells (individually hand-drawn and painted images) are required. Color photographs and illustrations.

Cartoon, Caricature, Animation
by Marcia Pointon, Published by Blackwell Publishers

Make Your Own Animated Movies & Videotapes; Film and Video Techniques from the Yellow Ball Workshop, Vol. 1
by Yvonne Andersen, Published by Little, Brown & Company

How to make animated movies including drawing the cartoon, operating the camera, and synchronizing the sound.

The Illusion of Life: Disney Animation
by Frank Thomas, Ollie Johnston, Published by Hyperiod

An out-of-print collector's item since 1986, the definitive account of the development of Disney animation explains what made Disney's style unique and features original sketches and drawings revealing the origins of Mickey and the rest.

Cartoon Animation Kit
by Walter Foster, Published by Walter Foster Publishing

Character construction and expression; line of action; two- and four-legged action cycles; and pose-planning techniques.

Encyclopedia of Animation Techniques: A Comprehensive, Step-by-Step Directory of Techniques
by Dick Taylor, Published by Running Press Book Publishers

From traditional cell animation to the most up-to-date computer animation, lighting, characterization, mixed media, and even puppet-making, the steps involved in going professional—from how animation studios operate to budgeting.

Animation: A Reference Guide
by Thomas W. Hoffer, Published by Greenwood Publishing Group, Incorporated

Art & Animation: Art & Design Profile 53
by Paul Wells (Editor), Published by Academy Ed

Cartoon Animation
by Preston Blair, Published by Walter Foster Publishing
A beginner's introduction to the fundamentals of drawing for the screen. Devotes particular attention to designing effective, engaging characters.

Christopher Hart's Portable Animation Studio
by Christopher Hart, Published by Watson-Guptill Publications
This fun-filled, full-color practice kit for aspiring animators contains an illustrated book, drawing pencil, a professional pencil test flip book, and two blank flip books. A great travel activity idea, this sturdy portfolio includes everything you need to get started. Full color.

Animator's Workbook: Step-by-Step Techniques of Drawn Animation
by Tony White, Published by Watson-Guptill Publications
Covers all the basics of animation technique. Includes techniques for in-betweener-level animators not included in more general books.

Animation from Script to Screen
by Shamus Culhane, Published by St Martins
A beginner's introduction to animation, going step-by-step through the process — not just from "script-to-screen," but from buying supplies to putting together a demo reel.

How to Draw Animation: Learn the Art of Animation from Character Design to Storyboards and Layouts
by Christopher Hart Published By Watson-Guptill
Not yet available.

The Artist's Complete Guide to Facial Expression
by Gary Faigin, Published by Watson-Guptill

A muscle-to-meaning approach to understanding how the human face communicates nonverbally. Essential for anyone doing character animation of any kind.

Flipbook Animation: And Other Ways to Make Cartoons Move
by Patrick Jenkins, Published by Can Press

An overall guide on creating animations. Includes instructions for creating drawings that give the illusion of various kinds of movement and special effects. Also describes several early motion picture devices.

Before the Animation Begins: The Art and Lives of Disney's Inspirational Sketch Artists
by John Canemaker, Published by Hyperion Books

For the first time ever, noted animation historian and animator John Canemaker documents the lives and works of Disney's "inspirational sketch artists" from the 1930s to the present.

Animated Cartoons: How They Are Made, Their Origin and Development
by Edwin George Lutz, Published by Applewood Books

One of the best books on the art of animation. Contains many shortcuts to animation, tips on drawing anatomy and motion along with how motion pictures are made and work.

Bugs Bunny: Fifty Years and Only One Grey Hare
by Joe Adamson, Friz Freleng, Chuck Jones, Published by Henry Holt and Company

This gloriously illustrated edition commemorating Bugs Bunny's fiftieth birthday, gives the inside account of Bug's creation, through his early stages of development, and into his prime.

That's All Folks: The Art of Warner Bros. Animation
by Steve Schneider, Ray Bradbury, Published by: Henry Holt and Company

Here is the first comprehensive record of the classic Warner Bros. cartoon studio. Detailed research of the studio along with interviews with the animated geniuses who breathed life and laughter in the Looney Tunes.

Tex Avery: King of Cartoons
by Joe Adamson, Published by Da Capo Press
An overview of the life and works of cartoon's great Tex Avery.

Chuck Jones: A Flurry of Drawings
by Hugh Kenner, Chuck Jones, Published by University of California Press
Creator of Roadrunner and Wile E. Coyote, master animator Chuck Jones has won three Academy Awards and been responsible for cartoon classics featuring Bugs Bunny, Elmer Fudd, and others. Now, A Flurry of Drawings reveals in cartoon-like sequences the irrepressible humor and profound reflection that have shaped Jones' work.

Chuck Reducks: Drawing from the Fun Side of Life
by Chuck Jones, Published by Warner Books
The world-renowned animation director of Bugs Bunny and Daffy Duck further shares his life, his inspiration, and his timeless creations in this charming and funny sequel to his treasured memoir, Chuck Amuck—with a Foreword, this time, by Robin Williams. Four 4-color inserts. Line art throughout.

Chuck Amuck: The Life and Times of an Animated Cartoonist
by Chuck Jones, Published by Farrar Straus & Giroux
A long line of animated mischief makers sprang from his pen: Bugs Bunny, Elmer Fudd, Daffy Duck, Wile E. Coyote, the Road Runner, Yosemite Sam, and countless others. He's Chuck Jones, one of the giants of animation, and his divinely daffy and unpretentious autobiography will delight readers with behind-the-scenes views of his life.

Cartooning the Head and Figure
by Jack Hamm Published by Perigee Books
Here are tried and proven methods that explain, simplify, and teach everyone, regardless of age, the art of cartooning. Step by step procedures with more than 3,000 illustrations.

Disney's Art of Animation: From Mickey Mouse to Beauty and the Beast
by Bob Thomas, Published by Hyperion

Thomas celebrates the magic of animation, explaining the basic techniques and giving examples of story sketches, layout animation drawings and background paintings—all the elements that go into the making of an animated film. With the cooperation of Walt Disney Productions, the publication of the book will tie in with the film Beauty and the Beast. 200 full-color illustrations.

Computer Animation/Digital Effects: General & Design

Character Animation in Depth
by Doug Kelly, Published by Ventana

Character animation is a high profile field with high salaries, high visibility tie-ins to TV and film, heavy recruiting, and few formal training requirements. This complete reference covers all key resources for character animation. Demos and sample files are contained on the CD-ROM, along with demo reel video clips and stills from major studios and individual artists.

The Art of 3-D Computer Animation and Imaging
by Isaac Kerlow, Published by John Wiley & Sons

This book is an indispensable reference for anyone (beginner to expert) wanting to create realistic characters in 3D. It covers almost every critical aspect of creating and animating digital characters. It contains individual sections on each major body part, as well as numerous modeling and animation techniques (including useful student exercises).

3-D Human Modeling and Animation
by Peter Ratner, Published by John Wiley & Sons

This book is an indispensable reference for anyone (beginner to expert) wanting to create realistic characters in 3D. It covers almost every critical aspect of creating and animating digital characters. It contains individual sections on each major body part, as well as numerous modeling and animation techniques (including useful student exercises).

Story: Substance, Structure, Style, and the Principles for Screenwriting
by Robert Mckee, Published by Harper-Collins

A noted screenwriter and educator presents a complete guide to the art of screenwriting, explaining how to develop a storyline, refining a work in progress, and other key aspects of creating works for film. The must have book on screenwriting.

Digital Illusion: Entertaining the Future With High Technology
by Clark Dodsworth (Editor), Published by Addison-Wesley Publishing Company

Combining traditional entertainment skills with advanced tools and methods in computer graphics and image processing, the producers of interactive games, multimedia networks, virtual reality environments, and theme park rides are reshaping one of the largest industries in the world. This book details the design and implementation of computer-based entertainment.

Computer Facial Animation
by Frederic I. Parke, Keith Waters, Published by A. K. Peters, Limited

Detailed guide to design, modeling and animation of faces, from understanding the anatomy of the face to modeling techniques.

Principles of Three-Dimensional Computer Animation
by Michael O'Rourke, Published by W. W. Norton & Company, Incorporated

The basics of 3D computer animation, now updated to reflect the latest advances in animation technology. New sections cover advanced modeling, rendering, and animating techniques, including expressions, blended surfaces, environment rendering, animation constraints, volumetric lights, and an expanded description of particle systems.

Let There Be Life!: Animating with the Computer
by Christopher W. Baker, Published by Walker & C (?)

A fascinating introduction to the world of computer animation explains how the computer has changed the world of film and television animation, using full-color clips from movies and ads to show how dinosaurs can come to life and dolls can move like humans.

Animation & Scientific Visualization
by R. A. Earnshaw, Published by Academic Press, Incorporated

Digital Character Animation
by George Maestri, Published by New Riders
Grounded in the basics of traditional cell animation, this book provides the essential information needed to create convincing computer-generated characters in 2D and 3D.

Digital Cinematography
by Ben de Leeuw, Published by Academic Press, Incorporated
The exciting new filmmaking technology used to create Toy Story is explored in this book. Ben de Leeuw, a freelance animator specializing in character animation and digital cinematography, examines the differences between virtual and real cinematography, as well as the benefits and deficits of the computer as a cinematic tool.

Industrial Light & Magic: The Art of Special Effects
by Thomas G. Smith, George Lucas,

3-D Computer Animation
by John Vince, Published by Addison-Wesley Publishing Company
A tutorial guide to current techniques for 3-dimensional computer animation that explains key concepts at a level requiring little mathematical background.

Animation Techniques
by Christopher D. Watkins, Stephen Marenka, Published by Academic Press, Incorporated
Providing a brief look at the beginnings and future of animation, and the key people/companies involved in its advancement, this book covers numerous application areas including medicine, architecture, 3D-CAD modeling, entertainment and virtual reality. It explains technical concepts pertinent to animation including the senses, physics of light, 3D graphics generation, and sound.

3DMadness!
by Michael Jones, Allen Wyatt, Published By Sams
3D Madness! includes lots of tips, tricks, and traps as well as a Top 100 Graphics Techniques featured in the text and referenced in a jump table on the inside front cover. The CD-ROM is filled with 3D software. The disk contains a subset of the material on the CD-ROM.

Industrial Light & Magic: Intro to the Digital Realm
by Mark Cotta Vaz, Patricia Rose, Published by Del Rey
  Describes the advances in digital technology that allowed George Lucas's Industrial Light and Magic studio to create the unique special effects for such movies as *Terminator 2*, *The Mask*, *Jurassic Park*, and *Forrest Gump*.

Best New Animation Design, Vol. 2 (Motif Design)
by Rita Street (Editor), Published by Rockport Pub

Special Effects in Film and Television
by Jake Hamilton, Published by Dorling Kindersley Publishers
  For the first time, special effects experts allowed a photographer to go behind the scenes to reveal the fascinating secrets of their work, step-by-step. In this explosive introduction to the world of illusion, young readers discover how Steven Spielberg created the dinosaurs for "Jurassic Park", how Jim Carrey's eyes popped out in "Mask", and how the spectacular arrival of alien spaceships was staged in "Independence Day". Full-color photos.

Movie Magic: Behind the Scenes With Special Effects
by Elaine Scott, Published By William Morrow & Co.
  From the imploding house in Poltergeist to the T-rex in Jurassic Park, the fascinating world of special effects come to life in this newest addition to Scott's popular behind-the-scenes series. Scott introduces the geniuses—some of who got their start in their teens—who create the visual, physical, and makeup effects for movies and TV.

Secrets of Hollywood Special Effects
by Robert E. McCarthy, Focal Press
  A behind the scenes look at Hollywood's special effects industry.

Special Effects Sourcebook
by Robert E. McCarthy, Published by Focal Press

What an Art Director Does: An Introduction to Motion Picture Production Design
by Ward Preston, Published by Silman-James Press
  What an Art Director Does is a comprehensive introduction to film and television art direction and production design. Starting with

a brief history of the field, Mr. Preston's lively, well-written text leads the reader through the ins and outs of all the responsibilities and duties that fall on the art director's shoulders. A wealth of information on preparing script breakdowns, research, design and presentation, scouting and working on locations, set design and construction, working as part of a team, and much more is coupled with examples drawn from the author's own experiences. This book is a must-read for all aspiring production designers and all filmmakers who desire a firm understanding of the physical process of film production.

What a Producer Does: The Art of Moviemaking (Not the Business)
by Buck Houghton, Published by Silman-James Press

Computer Animation/Digital FX - Software & Programming

Lightwave 3D 5 Character Animation F/X
by Doug Kelly, Published by Ventana Co.

How to produce complete character animations; step-by-step tutorials and examples, tips and tweaks, and a 16-page, four-color section. The companion CD-ROM includes popular plug-ins available for LightWave.

Adobe After Effects (Classroom in a Book)
by Adobe Systems Development Team
Hayden Books/Adobe Press

A tutorial to help users turn their Macs into post-production suites to create movies, animation, and professional effects for digital output using Adobe After Effects.

C for Windows Animation Programming
by Lee A. Adams, Published by Windcrest

The most popular types of high-speed computer animation—cel, behavioral, kinematic, 2-D, 3-D, real-time, and frame animation.

Models and Techniques in Computer Animation
by Nadia Magnenat-Thalmann, Daniel Thalmann (Editor), Published by:Springer-Verlag New York, Incorporated

Real-Time Animation Toolkit in C++
by Rex E. Bradford, Published by John Wiley & Sons, Incorporated

C++ tools and utilities, a C++ animation class library, a CD with the class library, code for the animation programming examples in the book, plus extra programs.

Graphics Programming & Animation
by Peder Jungek, Published by R & D Books

Assembly Routines for EGA/VGA Graphics

3D Studio Max F/X: Creating Hollywood-Style Special Effects
by Jon A. Bell, Published by Ventana Press

Animation, illusion, camouflage, illumination and simulation—this is the stuff 3D special effects are made of. And with this book, readers learn from a 3D Studio MAX expert—plunging into three-dimensional worlds from outer space to undersea. Users can then springboard into creating their own computer fantasies for video productions, multimedia and educational presentations. Includes online component.

Inside 3d Studio Max: Advanced Modeling & Materials
by Dave Espinosa-Aguilar, Joshua R. Andersen, Steve Burke, phi Miller
Published by New Riders

This is Volume 2 of the Inside 3D Studio Max series. This tutorial is for the serious 3D Studio MAX professional or student. The reference takes users beyond the intermediate functions of Modeling and the Material Editor to provide detailed information that cannot be found anywhere else. The CD provides models and textures illustrating the detailed tutorial in the book.

Algorithm Animation (ACM Distinguished Dissertations)
by Marc H. Brown, Published by MIT Press

A history of the topic and a description of the development of a system for creating and interacting with animations.

Windows Animation Programming with C++
by Michael Young, Published by Academic Press Inc

Introduction to the fundamentals of animation programming for Windows using C++.

3D Studio Max Fundamentals
by Michael Todd Peterson, Larry Minton, Frank Delise, Published by New Riders
>The basics of using 3D Studio MAX.

3D Studio Plugin Ref
by Tim Forcade, Published by New Riders
>Information about 3D Studio IPAS Plug-ins available from Yost Group, Schreiber Instruments, Digimation, and other companies.

Caligari Truespace 2 Bible
by Peter M. Plantec, Published by IDG Books Worldwide
>An overview of 3D graphics and trueSpace, visualizing 3D on a 2D surface, and more.

Mastering Three-D Studio, Vol. 2: Animation & Video Post
by Todd Payne, Published by New Era Press

Inside 3D Studio Max: Animation
by George Maestri, Sanford Kennedy, Ralph Frantz, Steve Burke, Jason Greene, Published by New Riders
Volume 3 of the Inside 3D Max series.

Fallingwater in 3D Studio: A Case Study & Tutorial
by Laura Sanchez, Al Sanchez, Published by:
High Mountain Press, Incorporated
>Learn to model, render, and animate, using Frank Lloyd Wright's Fallingwater as the model. Companion disk includes exercises.

Character Animation with 3D Studio Max
by Stephanie Reese, Published by Ventana Press
>How to make any kind of creature move realistically, or synthetically.

Instant Animation with Visual Basic
by Michele LeRoux, Published by Wrox, Inc.
>A techniques-based tutorial on graphics and animation in the latest release of Visual Basic.

Softimage Design Guide: Everything You Need to Master 3d Modeling and Animation with Microsoft's Soft Image

by Barry Ruff,Gene Bodio, Published by Ventana Press

This book teaches the 3D savvy reader the necessary skills to create commercial-quality animations and 3D models with Softimage. The authors have also included a special insider look at some of Softimage's coolest, most powerful, and least-known tools.

3-D Studio Max: Tutorials from the Masters

by Michele Bousquet, Published by Delmar Publishers

Soar to a new level of expertise with step-by-step tutorials that let you experience the techniques used by the masters. Readers will learn how top artists model and animate with 3D Studio MAX and unlock the animation potential of this powerful software. The CD-ROM includes ready-made models and materials for use in the tutorials, as well as models and AVIs from other MAX users.

Advanced Animation & Rendering Techniques

by Alan Watt, Mark Watt, Published by Addison-Wesley Publishing Company

An exposition of state-of-the-art techniques in rendering and animation. This book provides a unique synthesis of techniques and theory. Each technique is illustrated with a series of full-color frames showing the development of the example.

3D Studio Special Effects

by Jon A. Bell, Published by New Riders

The complete and behind-the-scenes guide to professional special effects. Readers learn all the amazing 3D studio techniques used in Hollywood. A CD-ROM includes flics and still images—everything readers need to create each special effect. Written by noted professional artists and animators. Includes advanced IPAS plug-in effects and use of third-party applications.

Animals & People: 3d Studio Tips & Tricks

by Michele Bousquet, Published by Delmar Publishers

3D Studio Hollywood & Gaming Effects; With Cdrom

by David Carder, Eric Chadwick, Rick Daniels, Tim Forcade, Published by New Riders

The trade secrets of top Hollywood and videogame artists and animators—with detailed instructions on creating a huge array of effects, all of which are illustrated from the first step to the finished result. CD is packed with valuable tools.

Animation and 3D Modeling on the Macintosh

by Don Foley,Melora Foley, Published By
Peachpit Press

This visual, instructional tool will guide novice and experienced animators through the exhilarating but often complex challenge of designing in 3D. More than 1,000 striking color illustrations show how the world's best modelers and animators create their work. The book also reveals how to use the best tools available in the leading software packages.

Lightwave Power Guide; The Definitive Guide to LightWave's Hidden Power

by Dan Ablan, Published by New Riders

This book is a visual guide to unleashing LightWave's true power. It breaks down the powerful high-end functions of LightWave, and presents them with simple explanations and visual examples.

Web Publisher's 3D and Animation Design Guide for Windows

by Mary Jo Fahey, Published by Ventana Press

A close-up look is given at how famous artists, Hollywood directors, and corporations are using 3D and animation in their work and on their Web sites.

Mastering 3d Studio: Modeling, Rendering, & Animation

by Jon M. Duff, William A. Ross, Published by PWS Publishers, Published by Peachpit Press

Intermediate level follow-up to "Animation and 3D Modeling on the Mac" by the same authors, including new material covering Windows applications.

Animation Tips & Tricks for Windows & Macintosh

by Don Foley, Melora Foley, Published by John Wiley & Sons, Incorporated

Advanced computer graphics techniques in animation and visualization, virtual environments, object-oriented programming in computer animation, shape interrogation, facial animation, animation in architecture, and human modeling in visualization.

New Trends in Animation & Visualization
by Daniel Thalmann, Published by John Wiley & Sons, Incorporated

Advanced computer graphics techniques in animation and visualization, virtual environments, object-oriented programming in computer animation, shape interrogation, facial animation, animation in architecture, and human modeling in visualization.

Visual Basic Animation Graphics Programming
by Lee A. Adams, Published by Windcrest

Leading-edge animation in the Windows programming environment. Covers the techniques of cell, behavioral, kinematic, 2-D, 3-D, real-time, and frame animation, common effects such as run-cycles, background pans, motion blur, adjustable timers, and more. 3.5" disk included.

Glass & Reflection: 3d Studio Tips & Tricks
by Michele Bousquet, Glenn Melenhorst, Published by Delmar Pubs

Morphing & Animation: 3d Studio Tips & Tricks
by Michele Bousquet,Glenn Melenhorst, Published by Van Nostrand Reinhold Computer

Technical Tips: 3d Studio Tips & Tricks
by Michele Bousquet, Published by Delmar Publishers

3D Studio for Beginners
by Jim Lammers, Steven Elliott, Michael Todd Peterson, Published by New Riders

This hands-on tutorial provides new users with the information they need to become professional 3D Studio Animators—with ease. Using helpful tips and strategies, users will get productive quickly and master this popular software application. CD-ROM provides all the files for the exercises and examples in the book, animations, and utility programs. Loaded with tips and expert insight for the new 3D Studio user. Provides answers to questions such as "What is Gamma Correction and how does it affect the way my animations look?" Includes full-color illustrations. Covers Release 4 for DOS.

Game Graphics in C++
by Len Dorfman, Published by Computing McGraw-Hill

Intermediate and advanced-level C graphics and animation programmers who want to crank their skills up a notch will find here everything they need to start programming re-usable graphics objects for dazzling animation and special effects using C++. The disk is packed with useful material, including demonstration programs and a complete C++ graphics library.

Computer Animation: Programming Methods and Techniques
by Julio Sanchez, Maria P. Canton, Published by Computing McGraw Hill

Low-level programming for animated graphics software.

Interactive Computer Animation
by Nadia Magnenat-Thalmann, Daniel Thalmann (Editors), Published by Prentice Hall

This book compiles the most recent advances and techniques in computer animation from experts from around the world to provide the most up-to-date and comprehensive coverage of all that is possible in developing artificial life. Includes articles on motion capture, morphing, facial animation, etc.

Web Publisher's 3D and Animation Design Guide for Macintosh
by Mary Jo Fahey, Published by Coriolis Group

Step-by-step instructions for using 3D graphics and animation on the Web, including VRML, Java, 3D-processed sound, animation, and more.

Building VRML Worlds
by Ed Tittel (Editor), Claire Sanders, Charlie Scott, Paul Wolfe, Published by Osborne McGraw-Hill

This book is a complete source for learning how to create the exciting realm of a virtual world. It is a hands-on, how-to guide using VRML technology that combines lucid discussions of object definition and creation techniques with tool tutorials and a thorough analysis of existing VRML resources.

Animation/Effects Industry: General

Cartoon Monikers: An Insight into the Animation Industry
by Walter M. Brasch, Published by Bowling Green

Serious Business: The Art & Commerce of Animation in America
by Stefan Kanfer, Published by Scribners
A humorous and thorough guide to the evolution of American film animation also explores the parallel changes in twentieth-century culture and politics, using everything from Walt Disney to Beavis and Butthead as examples.

From Mouse to Mermaid: The Politics of Film, Gender, and Culture
by Elizabeth Bell, Lynda Haas, Laura Sells, Indiana University Press
The history of one of America's best-loved success stories.

The Digital Multimedia Cross Industry Guide
by Philip V. W. Dodds, Published by Focal Press Focal Press

Employment Resources

3-D Graphics & Animation: From Starting up to Standing Out
by Mark Giambruno, Published by New Riders
Designed for those looking to break into the business, this tutorial and guide gives readers a broad overview of the 3-D marketplace. Offers practical, real-world tutorials that will have readers creating 3D graphics quickly

Taking the Leap: Building a Career as a Visual Artist
by Cay Lang, Published by Chronicle Books
This book teaches artists how to succeed in today's complex and competitive art world. Offering inside information on how to show at galleries, nonprofit spaces, and museums, as well a host, this behind-the-scenes look at the art world reveals how decisions are

made and what artists can expect and how they can create their own art scene on their own terms.

Digital Frontier: Job & Opportunity Finder
by Don Altman, Published by Moon Lake Media

Jobs of the 21st century—from Cyber Copy and Digital Talent Scout to Internet Web Page Designer—are contained in this guide.

Cartoon Animation: Introduction to a Career
by Milton Gray, Published by Lion's Den Pub

1998 Animation Industry Directory
by, Published by Animation

Using the Internet in Your Job Search: An Easy Guide to Online Job Seeking and Career Information
by Fred E. Jandt and Mary B. Nemnich, Published by Jist Works

Using the Internet in Your Job Search explains how to connect to theInternet, find job listings and research potential employers, use news groupsto get leads, adapt resumes to an electronic format, and capture reader attention in the first screen. Also valuable advice on issues of how to use e-mail to contact potential employers, legal and ethical issues of the e-mail job search, and the psychology of using the Internet.

3D Modeling & Animation Marketplace: The Definitive Guide to the Multimillion Dollar 3D Industry
by Andrew Reese, Published by Coriolis Group

Getting Ready for a Career As a Computer Animator
by Bill Lund, Published By Capstone Press

Careers in Multimedia: Roles and Resources
by Hal Josephson, Trisha Gorman, Published by Brooks/Cole Pub. Company

Multimedia industry players reveal in their own words how they got their jobs and what a day-in-the-life really looks like for jobs ranging from producers to designers, content creators to new media lawyers.

Game Developer's Marketplace

by Ben Sawyer, Alex Dunne, Tor Berg, Published by Coriolis Group Books

This hands-on "Marketplace" guide is packed with insider tips, techniques, resources, and time-proven advice from industry experts. Key topics featured include how to find jobs in the interactive gaming field, how to start your own game company, how to protect your ideas and creative properties, how to find talented people to work on your creations, how to design killer games, how to negotiate contracts that work, and much more.

Careers in Multimedia

by Ken Fromm, Editor, Published by ZD Press

This book covers everything readers need to know in order to find work (or find employees). It discusses the various roles involved with multimedia projects, describing each in details such as: experience needed, how to find work, how to find people to do the work, where to network, what resources to use, how to interview, and what skills are involved in each one.

References

American Institute for Graphic Arts. (2001). AIGA|Aquent survey of design salaries 2000. [Booklet]. Aquent: Author.

American Institute for Graphic Arts. (2002). [On-line] Available: http://www.aiga.org

Bay Area Multimedia partnership (BAMP), North Valley Private Industry
Council (NOVA), Reagan & Associates. (1997). A labor market analysis of the interactive digital media industry: Opportunities in multimedia. [Booklet]. U.S. Department of Labor: Author.

Belvin, M. E. (1989). Design through discovery: An introduction to art and design. New York, NY: Holt, Rinehart and Winston, Inc.

City of Los Angeles Private Industry Council, North Valley Private Industry Council (NOVA), Bay Area Multimedia Partnership (BAMP), and The Public Affairs Coalition of the Alliance of Motion Picture and Television Producers, and The PMR Group. (1997). Making digits dance: Visual effects and animation careers in the entertainment industry. [Booklet]. U.S. Department of Labor: Author.

Dane, J. (Speaker) (2000). New media careers for artists and designers questionnaire. (Audio Cassette-taped Interviews). Atlanta, GA: Faison, B. S. (Interviewer).

Entertainment Industry Development Corporation (2002). [On-line].
Available: http://www.eidc.com

Entertainment Careers (2002). [On-line]. Available: http://www.entertainmentcareers.cc
Gilbert, R. (1998). Living with art. Boston, MA: McGraw Hill.

Hoover, M. (Speaker) (2000). New media careers for artists and designers questionnaire. (Audio Cassette-taped Interviews). Atlanta, GA: Faison, B. S. (Interviewer).

Matis, E. (Speaker) (2000). <u>New media careers for artists and designers questionnaire.</u> (Audio Cassette-taped Interviews). Alpharetta, GA: Faison, B. S. (Interviewer).

McDermott, C. (Speaker) (2000). <u>New media careers for artists and designers questionnaire.</u> (Audio Cassette-taped Interviews). Alpharetta, GA: Faison, B. S. (Interviewer).

National Association of Schools of Art And Design (2001). <u>National association of schools of art and design: Directory.</u> Author: NASAD.

New Media Centers 2002. [On-line]. Available: http://www.newmediacenters.org

The PMR Group (2002). [On-line]. Available: http://www.thepmrgroup.com

SkillsNet (2002). [On-line]. Available: http://www.skillsnet.net/core.cfm

Wong, W. (1993). <u>Principles of form and design.</u> New York, NY: John Wiley & Sons, Inc.

Zelanski, P., and Fisher M. P. (1994). <u>The art of seeing.</u> Englewood Cliffs, NJ: Prentice Hall, Inc.

Index

About the Author

Dr. Faison is president and founder of Brenda Faison and Associates, a multidisciplinary design firm headquartered in Richmond, Virginia. She has 19 years of combined design agency and design education experience. Her accounts include: GTE, GlaxoSmithKline, NorTel, L'eggs Products, and IBM, to name a few.

Over a five-year period, she worked with corporate giant IBM, both in Research Triangle Park, North Carolina (Design Center, Publications, and Marketing Solutions), and in Manassas, Virginia (Graphics and Presentations).

For twelve years Dr. Faison has taught design and new media on the university level within a variety of disciplines including Visual Arts, Art Education, Computer Science, Information Systems, and Mass Communications. She received her doctorate in Computer Graphics Technologies from The Ohio State University at Columbus, studying at its Advanced Computing Center for the Arts and Design (ACCAD); and has earned professional certificates in Web and Multimedia Development from the Georgia Institute of Technology, in Atlanta, Georgia.

Dr. Faison is a member of the Phi Kappa Phi Honor Society, the Association for Computing Machinery (ACM), ACM SIGGRAPH, and the Association for Education in Journalism and Mass Communication (AEJMC).

Notes

Notes

Notes

Printed in the United States
29091LVS00005B/254

9 781403 356468